Text Copyri
The moral rights of the author have been asserted.

Cover photograph: Dorothy 1934

First Edition – October 2009

Main text set in 12 point Garamond

ISBN 978-1-4452-1317-0

A Dot's Life
By Dorothy Buchanan

The autobiography of a
girl growing up in Liverpool
in the Thirties and Forties

Volume One
1934-1946

To Mike,

*My soul-mate.
I am so glad that we found each other.
This book is for you with all my love
and appreciation.*

Dot

Preface

This first volume covers the years between 1934 and 1946, which includes a young girl growing up in second world-war Britain, a teenager finding her feet in the world of work, and a young woman starting to date.

Since all the material is autobiographical, and therefore subjective, I have made every effort to be accurate in detail as well as emotion.

The second volume will cover my early married life and the beginnings of my own family.

I hope you enjoy this first volume!

Dot

buchanandorothy@yahoo.co.uk

Contents

6	*A note on the Family Tree*
7	*The Family Tree*
9	Us or them
13	A House is not a Home
21	New Brighton and New Arrival
28	Grandma Phillips and the Clay Pipe
32	Daisy and the Bridesmaid
37	Clean up and Tea time
44	We Interrupt this Programme...
49	The Shelter in the Cellar and the College
60	Mailer, Scraps and Fruit
65	A letter for Dad and Chores for Me
68	Mailer and the Adoption Papers
71	Burma and Parcels for Dad
74	Jean's Secret and Uncle Leslie's Illness
78	Uncle Leslie's Farewell
81	Miss Schneider and the Job Hunt
89	Fortune Telling and Hairdressing
96	Eric, the Witch and the Walk home
101	Herbie Rides Again
106	Ingrid Bergman in Aunty Mary's Nightdress
110	From Fairgrounds to Battlegrounds
119	One Good Assault Leads to Another
126	Tea Leaves and Nylon Stockings
131	Mike, Terry and the Crocodile
137	A Handbag, but not Crocodile
141	Milly's Secret and Another World
151	In Touch
159	The Luck of the Irish
166	Sugar and Spice and All Things Nice
172	A Last Supper
176	Crucifixion and Burial
178	High Heels and Flats
183	To Pin a Sin on Tim
188	A Little Bit of Powder
192	Steve Goes Fishing
196	To Hook a Duck
201	The Lunch Box

A note on the family tree overpage

This family tree includes only those family members directly referred to in the text.

Because this volume covers the period between 1934 and 1946, it does not yet include my husband, Mike (to whom this is dedicated) or my five children, Avram, Julian, Nick, Sharon and Jane – all of whom deserve a mention. Each is special. But this volume is before their time.

I hope that the diagram overpage gives you, the reader, a richer experience and a clearer understanding of the families Phillips and Lawrence.

It is perhaps worth emphasizing also that one's life is shaped, not only by family, but also by friends, teachers, colleagues, youth workers, etc.

For better or worse, we become the sum of what we do with all of our experiences.

A Dot's Life by Dorothy Buchanan

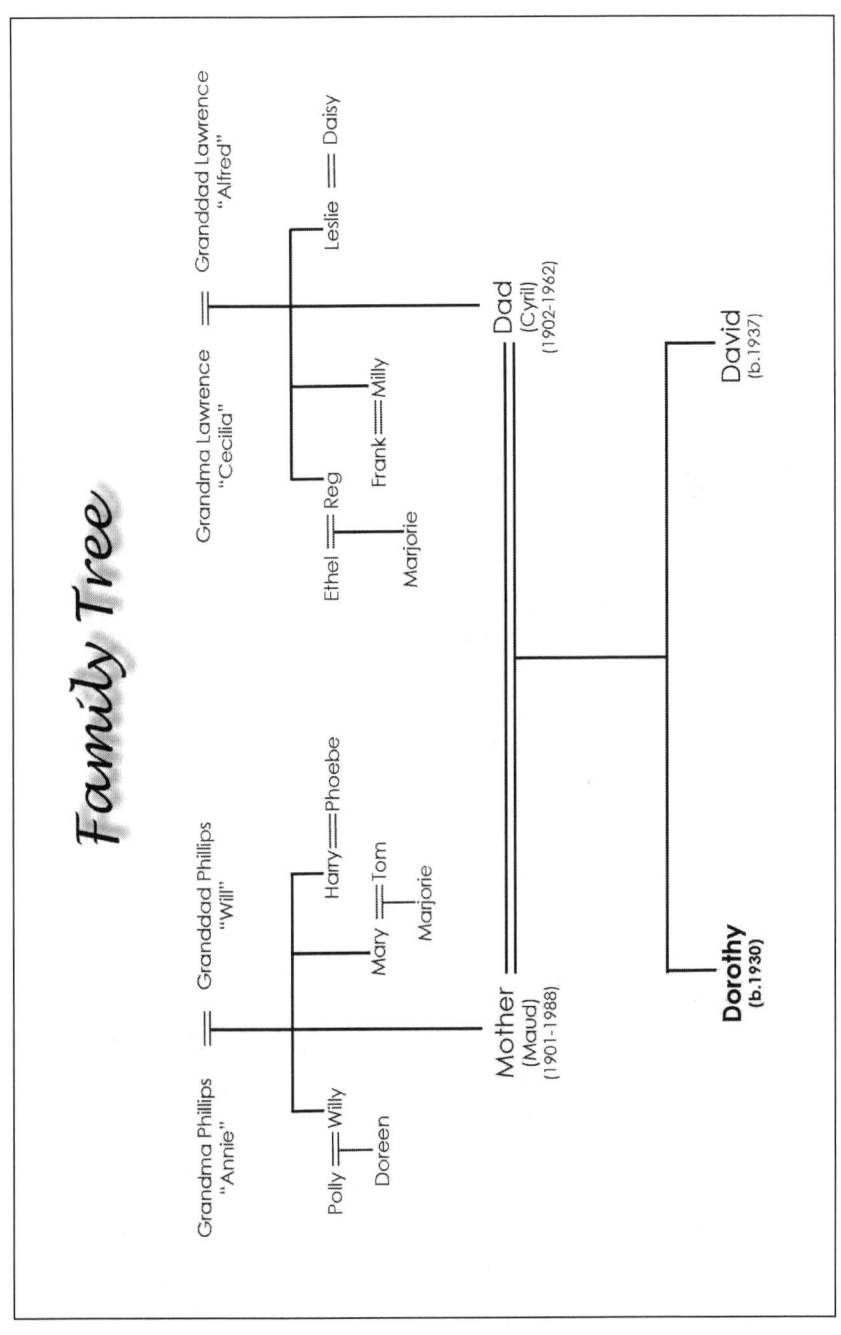

A Dot's Life by Dorothy Buchanan

Chapter One
Us or them

I was almost five when we moved to a ground floor flat in Faulkner Street, Liverpool. Once there, we quickly realised we were overrun with cockroaches, especially in the kitchenette. Each time we switched on the light, a black mass of them would scurry out of sight, but there would always be the few that weren't quick enough!

I used to help Dad kill as many as we could with the back of a wooden scrubbing brush, it became quite a game, their black shiny shells would pop, and out would ooze a horrible white puss-like substance. Some would get into our shoes overnight it became a habit with everyone to bang them before putting them on!

Everyone seemed to have cockroaches, but for some reason nobody appeared to know how to get rid of them; they simply multiplied and were accepted as a fact of life.

I refer to it as a flat – but perhaps 'flat' is the wrong word - rooms - would be more appropriate. There was a living room at the front of the house - and along the hallway, a bedroom, which I shared with my mother and father. Our tiny kitchenette under the stairs had only enough room for a small cooker, a sink and cupboard for food.

Nobody used the communal bathroom on the first floor for bathing. The bath, once white, was now chipped black with orange rust eating it away, and the brass taps were green with furred verdigris. The lavatory, once an ornate item, was now reduced to a dull brown seat with two channels of grease where legs had sat. The pan, a grey veil of cracks was stained with years of urine but the outside had a blue floral decoration, which seemed to be trying to redeem past glory.

The flat dwellers used the lavatory frequently, but we all kept a bucket in our bedrooms for urinating. Morning and evening, there

A Dot's Life by Dorothy Buchanan

would always be someone emptying their bucket; the linoleum floor was always sticky. Nobody ever cleaned it, it smelt dreadful!

Opposite our house lived a Chinese family and I played with their daughter. I don't remember her name, but their home made a big impression on me, it was like entering another world. The walls were painted dark red and a shiny silk material decorated with dragons, draped one wall. There were pictures of Chinese landscapes, photographs of elderly relatives, paper lanterns with gold tassels, and beaded curtains covered the doors.

The floor was strewn with large red and gold embroidered cushions and the furniture, mostly black ebony, consisted of very low tables. It also smelt strange, but not unpleasant. A large ornament of a Chinese gentleman, similar to a Sumo wrestler took pride of place on the window ledge. I never saw any men in the house - perhaps they went to sea? My friend, her mother and her sister all looked the same, with short black hair and heavy fringes to their eyes. Their mother and sister wore kimonos and raffia sandals.

The atmosphere in the house was always very peaceful and serene, they seemed to glide around treading very softly; their expressions were always the same, neither pleased nor irritated. I often enjoyed eating a bowl of rice with them, using my fingers! Only my little friend spoke English.

The house next door to ours was occupied by an elderly lady and her maid. Sometimes when I saw the elderly lady she would give me a chocolate biscuit wrapped in silver paper, it was quite a luxury. I'd never seen a wrapped biscuit until then, as biscuits were sold loose from glass fronted tins in grocery stores. Most people we knew bought broken biscuits, as they were much cheaper.

Prior to this Flat, we lived in one of a long row of grey stoned houses, in St. James's Road opposite Liverpool's Anglican Cathedral. We lived in number fourteen, my parents being the caretakers of this three storey house. Black ornate railings and stone steps at the front led to our basement entrance; the rest of the house contained private apartments, which were entered by the

A Dot's Life by Dorothy Buchanan

large black front door.

I don't remember seeing any of the tenants, except for an old man who occupied the attic - his name was Mr Grooby. Mother told me I visited him often. A cluttered dark dusty room springs to mind, and a tall backed chair, where the bulky man sat. Was he a lonely old man I wonder, who enjoyed the chatter of a four year old - or did he have other intentions? I have no recollections.

At that time, around 1934, Mother's work occupied most of the day and I was usually in the care of local older girls. I remember being taken by them to play inside the Cathedral. We'd play hide and seek, or go to the adjoining St James's Cemetery which was overgrown and lush with shrubs and ivy. We would run down the winding entrance where carriages with black plumed horses had once brought the dead, then spend our time looking for the spring which was in the centre somewhere. When we were fortunate enough to find it, we'd remove our shoes and socks and splash about there for ages. Most days were spent this way.

My father was a joiner and worked for a furniture company called Waring & Gillows, in Liverpool city centre, but as with most work places then, the wages were very poor. He was looking for a better paid job and managed to obtain one as a caretaker to a large Church opposite the famous Philharmonic Hall. The Church, called 'Myrtle Street Baptist Church', was a very stately building and quite large. His role as caretaker was an almost impossible task! He was a full-time cleaner, with one thousand rexine tip-up seats to clean, floors to be brushed and woodwork to be polished (including the pulpit, pews and doors). His responsibilities included the window cleaning, every minor repair, painting and decorating and he also had to attend to the boiler. Consequently each days' work would last until early evening.

In 1935 I began school at St. Margaret's in Princes Road, not far from where we lived. It was a High Church of England school, with a Church attached. I enjoyed school very much, except for the amount of time we spent attending church.

Father Marshall conducted numerous services for Saint days, for which there was an endless supply! Lots of children sitting in the front seats often fainted, perhaps with the strong smell of incense? On Ash Wednesday ashes would be smeared across our foreheads, which for some reason made us feel rather special. St. Margaret's was considered a good school and was attended by children of different religions and nationalities as it was then, and still remains, a very cosmopolitan area.

A penny a week had to be paid by each pupil for School Maintenance. I became friendly with two girls who began school with me, Elsie Casey and June Furlong. Elsie was fair haired and sunny natured, we giggled a lot and enjoyed similar things. June was a pretty girl, rather fragile looking and quite small for her age. She always came to school looking as if she was going to a party. Her light brown hair dressed in ringlets, with fancy ribbons and her clothes the envy of most of the children, Elsie and I included!

Chapter Two
A House is not a Home

On our way to school one morning, while walking along Bedford Street, Mother noticed a removal van outside a house in Egerton Street, a side street with garden fronted terraced houses. She noticed a well dressed man at the door and presumed he must be the landlord collecting the final weeks rent. Most people rented houses, only rich people owned their own. Mother rushed me up the street to catch him and after a quick few words she was showing him her rent book and giving him money. She'd become red and flustered;

"It's a good job I had my rent book with me," she gasped "And enough money for two weeks rent, otherwise he'd have let someone else have that house!" I didn't understand what she was talking about.

"That's our house now," she said excitedly, rushing me along. I didn't reply, I was more worried about being late for school! I soon became excited though, once I realised we were now moving to a house of our own!

Boxes began to get filled (the flat was piled high with them) and Mother and Dad seemed busy all the time packing and planning everything. Within a week a big furniture van arrived and I stayed away from school that day. When the removal men suggested I ride with them in the front seat, I was delighted - I'd never been in a car let alone a big van before! Sitting between the two burly men was very exciting! I kept wishing I'd see someone I knew, so I could give them a wave!

Mother was already in the house when we arrived and the front door was wide open. I ran along the long hallway. Two doors led off to a front parlour and living room, with a flight of stairs at the end. It seemed huge, after the flats we'd lived in. The living room led into a small kitchen with a door to the backyard and an outside lavatory and it also had a cellar to keep the coal. Upstairs, there were two bedrooms and a bathroom, which contained a bath but

A Dot's Life by Dorothy Buchanan

no lavatory or wash basin - but the bath was white with no chips or rust. I was intrigued to notice a door along the landing which I thought to be a cupboard, but it opened to a flight of winding stairs, leading to an attic with a skylight window. I fell in love with everything, even the tiny front garden with its colourful flowers and shrubs and the front iron gate with the tiny path leading to our front door.

We soon settled in our new home but more furniture was badly needed. This was solved quite quickly with endless trips to second-hand shops; a couple of easy chairs, a chest of drawers and single bed for my bedroom, some mirrors and a wireless.

On Saturday evenings we would go to "Paddy's Market" in Cazeneu Street, a rough area of Liverpool that sold lots of bargains, we bought cheap linoleum and rugs for the floors which were sold from the back of big vans. Dad had to carry everything home over his shoulders; it took quite a few Saturday trips as there were a lot of floors to cover. Every bit of his spare time would be spent painting or wallpapering.

Fortunately, lots of children lived in Egerton Street and I quickly made friends. I spent most days after school playing in the street. There was no fear of traffic as there weren't many cars in side streets. The only disruption to our play was when the Coal man or Bin men came. They would drive their horses and carts up every street. Occasionally Rag and bone men would come shouting for old clothes and household items and if you gave them old clothes they would reward you with a toy or goldfish in a jam jar, but the poor fishes never lived long.

I regularly had to go errands as most children did, Mother usually sent me for milk or bread, which were sold at a corner shop. I hated going to the butchers in Myrtle street - not only was it a long walk but I always found it difficult remembering the message. Mother often asked me to buy "Lean loin chops" and I used to chant "Lean-loin-chops-lean-loin-chops" to myself all the way there!

The chore I disliked most was taking the accumulator each week to be charged at the local garage. The wireless worked with this square shaped thick glass vessel containing acid. It had a thick metal handle inserted in the glass and was very heavy too. I was always frightened of dropping it, but fortunately I never did.

We played lots of games in the street; rounders, tennis, cricket (using the same tennis ball) the bat for each game was crudely made from a piece of wood. We'd skip with a thick rope spread across the street, and it was very heavy, if you were unlucky enough to get a lash from it, your leg would sting for ages! I imagine it came from the docks.

We played marbles which we'd roll along the gutters. We kept them in little drawstring bags, the prize ones were coloured with milky stripes. Most of the boys were very good at winning them from the girls so we tried not to play with *them*.
The back entry's were broad enough to play lots of games, some people hung their washing across them, although Mother never did. More often than not, we played our games in the front street much to the annoyance of our next door neighbour, Mrs. Edge. She always seemed to be shouting at us for something or other,
"Stop making so much noise" or "Don't play ball around here" None of the other neighbours ever complained. I didn't like her. None of us took much notice of her.

Mother didn't bother with any of our neighbours, except for Mrs Edge. She seemed to get on with her very well, they would often have long chats with each other on the front step. Mother said she was very "respectable", unlike most of the other neighbours! Mrs Edge took a keen interest in the coming and going of the rest of the street. Not much happened without her knowing about it. I imagine this is what they talked about! A lot of my friends Mothers said she was "A nosy hole" but I never told Mother. Her husband sat by the parlour window all day reading, dozing or eating. Mrs Edge told Mother he was an invalid, but there didn't seem much wrong with him.

One afternoon we spotted Mrs Edge going shopping and decided to play rounders uninterrupted in the front street, we were quite

A Dot's Life by Dorothy Buchanan

involved in our game when Jean, one of my friends, stopped playing and shouted "Hey! Look at Mr. Edge" We all looked towards his front window. Sure enough there was Mr. Edge standing up this time, not looking angry as I expected, but grinning and shaking himself about. We ran into the tiny front garden to have a better look, for a moment or two we stood and stared opened mouthed, we'd never seen anything like it before, Mr. Edge was exposing himself!

"Dirty bugger" hissed Jean, she liked using swear words. She ran to his front door and opened the letter box and shouted *"Dan, Dan, you're a dirty old man!"* We all thought this great fun and each one of us did the same. He removed himself from the window quite quickly. We talked and laughed about it for ages afterwards, but none of us told our parents of the event, neither of course did Mr. Edge tell his wife. Although we kept a watchful eye on the Edge's front window, we never saw him there again!

Another house further down the road became far more interesting, especially to the girls. It was occupied by two young women who were very glamorous; one had black hair, the other blonde; ("Peroxide Blonde" as it was called!). Each wore heavy make-up, lovely clothes high heeled shoes and silk stockings with black seams, they looked like film stars we all admired them. To add to our pleasure, they were very generous when we went errands for then. They would say "Keep the change love" which would be far more than we received from anyone else, sometimes as much as a shilling!

They had lots of visitors too, mostly Chinese men who arrived in black taxis. I thought they must be very popular, with so many friends calling so regularly. I mentioned to mother how lovely I thought they both were, she almost exploded-

"Lovely?" She screamed. "Those women are no good. Don't you ever go anywhere near that bad house. Do you understand?" Her anger alarmed me, I just nodded. When I related mothers' outburst to Jean, she didn't seem at all surprised-

"Well they are prostitutes, *everyone* knows that!" I hadn't any idea what prostitutes were, but I tried to look knowledgeable.

A Dot's Life by Dorothy Buchanan

Far from keeping away from the "Bad house" it now held more fascination than ever. We still went messages for them, but I was careful not to let mother see. We often watched the numerous visitors, and amused ourselves, guessing how long each would stay. One afternoon they asked Jean and I to go for a bottle of milk, as usual they told us to keep the change. We took quite a long time choosing which sweets to buy.

"They'll think we're lost, come on lets hurry up " Jean laughed. When we returned to their house the front door was ajar, we knocked repeatedly but nobody answered.

"Go on in, here's your chance to see what it's like inside" Jean whispered giving me a push. Even though I was apprehensive, I didn't need much persuading. I pushed open the door gingerly, then, quietly crept along the bare hall to the closed living room door. Slowly I turned the handle and went in. The light in the room was very dim and the curtains were closed, folds of grey smoke hung over the heads of two Chinese men who sat cross legged on a bare mattress. Both were smoking long pipes. They stared at me, but didn't appear to see me.

"Here's the milk" I said in almost a whisper, neither of them moved a muscle, their fixed gaze concentrated on me. I felt frightened. Glancing through the smoky haze, I noticed the room contained no other furniture at all. The strange smell in the room was quite overpowering. I placed the bottle of milk on the floor, and made my way along the hall and out into the street as fast as I could.

Jean was waiting anxiously to hear all the news.

"Well," she said in anticipation. "What's it like in there?"

"My Mam says it's probably filthy." I told her all I had seen.

"I'll bet that was Hash they were smoking. My Dad says those Chinese seamen bring it from China, and it stinks. That would be what the smell was." I was very popular that day, everyone wanted to know what the Bad house was like inside!

I saw Jean most days, I thought of her as my best friend. She was a great organizer and had opinions about everything. I liked her very much; she was popular with everyone. She lived in a house much larger than ours at the end of the street. They had a big family and all of the children were older than her. Some were married but still lived at home, with their partners and babies.

It upset me, when Mother referred to her as "The girl from that rough family." She believed all big families were rough and she would have preferred me not to associate with her at all! The atmosphere in their house was so different to ours. They would ask me in whenever I called for Jean, if they were having a meal they'd insist I had something to eat with them, usually a thickly cut jam buttie and a cup of strong sweet tea. They made me feel like one of the family, I loved being there.

Mother wouldn't allow me to invite any of my friends to our house. She'd have been very angry if she'd known I went into Jean's house. She would have been horrified too, had she seen how they lived; a newspaper tablecloth, cracked or chipped cups with no handles, a bag of sugar, a jar of jam, margarine in its wrapper, a bottle of milk, all on the table throughout the day. But it seemed happy and homely to me. It was always untidy - clothes would be left lying around and they were always hunting for missing socks and shoes! These things never appeared to bother any of them. They laughed and joked with each other, even their Mother and Father joined in. I often wished we could be like that. Mother and Dad certainly never joked or laughed very much. Life and living in our house seemed a serious business.

Jean's father was a docker and usually after work he'd sit at the table eating his evening meal in his vest and trousers. I was fascinated by his numerous tattoos. He was a big lively man who loved making people laugh. He told endless jokes and sometimes Jean and I wouldn't understand them but we'd laugh, just the same.
Mother wouldn't allow Dad to sit in his vest.
  "Only common people behaved like that!" She'd say.

Mother had been in service with the same family from the age of thirteen, and even married from her employers' house when she was twenty seven. Much to her surprise and dismay I was born ten months later!

A Dot's Life by Dorothy Buchanan

Now Mother at last had a house of her own and not rooms or flats, she emulated her employers' manners and routines. Every morning she said she had her "Duties" to attend to. She never called it housework. Each day had a particular job which had to be done at all costs. The house was kept spotless and tidy. In the afternoon, her working clothes would be replaced with a dress and frilly apron, and then she would become the lady of the house! She insisted on an orderly routine with everything.

I often went with my father to work in the church. He seemed different when we were on our own, somehow more relaxed and friendly and I always enjoyed those times. While he got on with his numerous jobs, I amused myself either standing in the pulpit, giving imaginary sermons to empty seats, or wandering tiptoe around the vast unlit cellars. I enjoyed frightening myself, thinking something or someone unknown might jump out on me. I loved the damp dank smell it had too. It reminded me of a railway station.

One job I helped Dad with, was preparing the Communion tray. Stale bread without any crusts had to be neatly cut into tiny squares and then arranged on a silver platter. Small wine glasses had to be half filled with red wine, I often took a slurp of wine when Dad wasn't looking, I didn't like it much, but I felt quite daring. I hadn't any idea what Communion was - it seemed strange to me eating stale bread and drinking wine. With Dad being the caretaker it was expected that I attend church services each Sunday, which I hated.

Mother visited her mother, Grandma Phillips, a few times a week. She didn't live near to us but mother always walked there, which took about half an hour. Sometimes she hadn't arrived home, when I came from school.

"If I'm not in when you get home, go around the back and wait in the lavatory" she reminded me daily.

These occasions happened regularly. I was always pleased when she'd left me a couple of jam butties wrapped in brown paper - on the lavatory seat! After eating them I went in the street to play, but if it was raining I had to sit there until she came home. I got very

A Dot's Life by Dorothy Buchanan

bored and sometimes to amuse myself, I'd light the candle that was left for nightly visits to the lavatory, and burn bits of newspaper that had been cut into squares for toilet paper. If I had any sweets I'd try and roast them over the flame, but they usually tasted awful. I hated those long waits in the lavatory!

Arriving from school one day when Mother was home, I noticed the parlour door ajar. The door was usually kept closed because the room wasn't furnished. There inside I saw a huge black pram.

"Who does that belong to?" I enquired, pushing the door open to get a closer look. It had tiny black wheels and a big black boat shaped body even inside the hood was black. I'd never seen a pram like it before. It was very big, ugly and old fashioned.

"I'm looking after it for a friend" Mother said.

"Well, keep the parlour door closed, in case anyone thinks it's ours," I shouted. I couldn't imagine who would want such an ugly pram for their baby. It was never mentioned again. I thought Mothers' friend must have taken it, as the parlour door was always closed!

Chapter Three
New Brighton and New Arrival

It was now May 1938 and a time in the year when the days were getting warmer. I spent most of my time after school playing in the street with my friends. Occasionally on Saturdays, if Dad wasn't required at the church, he and Mother would take me on a day trip. We didn't go very far, usually to New Brighton, a popular seaside resort across the River Mersey.

I loved going on the ferry, but mother was seasick every time, although the journey was only half an hour. If the tide was out when we arrived, we would go on the beach and Dad would get Mother a deck chair, then he'd take me on the rocks by the lighthouse to find crabs. I loved those times. Dad seemed to enjoy looking for crabs or unusual pebbles as much as me. I always longed to have fish and chips while we were there and eat them from the paper walking along the promenade, like most people did, but Mother wouldn't hear of it.

"I wouldn't be seen dead walking down a street, eating fish and chips from the paper! Anyway, I've brought plenty of sandwiches"

"But lots of people do when they're at the seaside," I insisted. "I hate sandwiches. You always make those terrible meat paste ones!"
Mother became angry.

"Well that settles it" she said "You're not having any. I'll teach you not to be so cheeky." After she and Dad ate some she put the rest back in her bag.
As the day wore on I became very hungry and asked reluctantly for a sandwich.

"You'll have to ask me properly," she said.
Dad intervened "Oh give her one love, she must be hungry"
But Mother was adamant," Not until she asks me properly!"
Dad didn't say anything this time. I knew I would have to ask her the way she demanded, but the words stuck in my throat.

"Please may I have a sandwich" I asked through clenched

A Dot's Life by Dorothy Buchanan

teeth. I was given two rather dry curly sandwiches, but I was still hungry.

Much to my surprise, one afternoon Grandma Phillips answered the door to me when I arrived home from school. This was most unusual as she only visited us at Christmas time.

"Sorry to keep you waiting love," she said breathlessly. "It took me a time to get down the stairs." She put her arm around me hugging me close, and whispered "Go upstairs and see what your Mother has for you"

I ran upstairs as fast as I could feeling very excited, maybe at last she'd got me the bike? I was always asking for one - or even roller skates? I couldn't get up the stairs quick enough. There was nothing in my bedroom. I ran into Mother and Dad's room. Pushing the door open wide, I was amazed to see Mother in bed. But there was no bike or skates to be seen. I was puzzled. Mother was propped up, with her back to me, before I could say anything Grandma pushed me towards her.

"Look," she said pointing the other side of Mother. "You've got a little brother; aren't you a lucky girl?" I was stunned. I couldn't believe what I was hearing.

"We're so lucky to have him too," continued Grandma, looking lovingly towards the baby.

"The doctor had to give him brandy and water and wrap him in cotton wool to keep him alive, but thank God he's alright now!" I was shocked, I couldn't speak.

"We are going to call him David George" said Mother turning towards me for the first time. "George, being your Dad's second name." I wasn't interested what he was going to be called. Grandma smiled and stroked the baby's head.

"He'll grow up to be a Goliath, I'll bet," she said.

I looked at the baby lying beside Mother. He looked awful, not like a baby at all. He had no eyelashes or eyebrows. His yellow crinkled face looked old and his tiny stick-like arms were waving about aimlessly. I thought he was horrible, I hated him! The last thing I wanted was a baby in the house!

"Well," asked mother proudly. "What do you think of your little brother?" Tears were sprouting from my eyes. I felt cheated and angry.

A Dot's Life by Dorothy Buchanan

"He's no brother of mine," I said defiantly. I couldn't bear to look at him anymore. "In fact he's no relation of mine at all." I shouted, rushing out of the room and down the stairs. I could hear Grandma and Mother laughing at my remarks as I sat on the bottom stair, quietly sobbing. I felt I'd never get over this shock.

After a while I went out to play. I told Jean about my disappointment of finding we had a baby, she was amazed

"Your Mother's had a baby? Gosh, she kept that quiet didn't she? But babies are lovely. I've seen all the new born ones in our street, go and ask your Mother if I can I can see yours".

I ran home to ask Mother, feeling more at ease with things now. Mother was adamant "I'm not having that sort of girl in here breathing germs everywhere. She'll be able to see him when he's taken out in his pram." Oh no! That was another blow, I'd forgotten about that horrendous pram. It was ours after all!

Life at home was very different now, there seemed to be endless feeding sessions and nappies everywhere, either in buckets soaking or drying by the fire. David cried a lot and Mother became very irritable. She shouted at me for the least thing. Nothing I did pleased her - even Dad annoyed her.

I kept out of the way as much as I could. I had no interest in David and hated the disruption he'd caused. I was appalled when Mother insisted I take him a walk each day after school - in that awful pram too! I dreaded that. I knew all my friends would laugh at such a monstrosity. That first day out with David in the pram was very embarrassing - it seemed as if all the children from the street were out playing. They took one look at the pram and screeched with laugher, just as I'd imagined.

"Where did you get that pram?" they giggled

"Did your mother get it off Queen Victoria?" One of the lads shouted.

I felt awful and tried to smile. "It looks like it doesn't it," I said putting on a brave face, but I hoped they wouldn't mention it again. David was scrutinised by all of them but thankfully no comments were made about him.

23

A Dot's Life by Dorothy Buchanan

Mother was concerned about Grandma. She hadn't been able to make her regular visits since David was born.

"You'll have to go to Grandma's now," she said one afternoon. "You could go every Saturday and do a few jobs and messages for her." I was angry. Doing jobs and messages was not my idea of fun. I made a lot of protests but it was no use, I still had to go.

The following Saturday morning I made my way to Grandma's feeling very sorry for myself. I'd hoped to make the journey by tram car, but mother said the walk would do me good.

Grandma and Granddad Phillips' lived in a tiny four roomed terraced house in Alfred Street, in the Wavertree area of Liverpool. It had no bathroom, just a lavatory which was in the backyard. The house inside and out was badly neglected and needed lots of repairs. When I arrived, Grandma was making herself a pot of tea. She was surprised.

"Hello Dolly. I didn't expect to see you, but I'm glad of a bit of company," she said welcoming me into the living room. "Before you take your coat off will you run a message for me?" I nodded. She took some money from her apron pocket and tore a piece of newspaper to wrap it in.

"Go to Irwin's and get me a fruit malt loaf, half a pound of broken biscuits and a quarter of best butter, then we can tuck in, with our cup of tea."

I glanced around her tiny living room, so different from our immaculately kept home. The sideboard was cluttered with an assortment of things; medicine bottles, insurance books, tins of ointment, rolled up stockings, a dusty Aspidistra. The old horse hair couch under the window was missing a leg and was propped up with a large biscuit tin. The green chenille cloth on the table looked stained and grimy - I hoped Grandma wouldn't ask me to clean this room. I brought back the groceries with a heavy heart, dreading the rest of the day.

Two cups of steaming tea were waiting on the table when I got

A Dot's Life by Dorothy Buchanan

back from the shopping.

"Come on Dolly take off your coat and sit down, help yourself to sugar."

She pulled a chair to the table for me.

"If your Mother heard me calling you "Dolly" she'd have a fit wouldn't she?" she laughed. "But she's not here, so she won't know!" While she talked, she spread butter thickly on slices of fruit malt bread. I was hungry after the long walk. We ate in silence. I enjoyed sinking my teeth into each slice. We finished the loaf in no time, then started on the biscuits, still in the bag. I noticed she dipped hers into her tea, something Mother would never allow. I did the same. I was beginning to enjoy myself, after all.

Grandma poured herself a second cup of tea, then from her apron pocket produced a white clay pipe, stuffed it with tobacco and lit it. I was astonished my mouth was gaping open. I never knew ladies smoked pipes. I just stared at her in silence. As she puffed on her pipe, she told me lots of stories about her life in Stone in Staffordshire were she'd lived as a girl. She said she hardly ever went to school.

"I was too valuable at home," she said, and then went on to tell me gory details of how she had to catch, kill and skin rabbits, pluck pigeons and chickens and drown unwanted kittens. It all sounded dreadful to me and very cruel, but I thought it best not to make any comments.

Tears came to her eyes as she talked about her two sons who had died. The eldest Willy, who had been gassed in the First World War, was only thirty three, and the younger Harry, aged twenty eight, became so poor after he married, he died of malnutrition.

"Nobody knew how hard up he was," she said in hushed tones. "But still, I've got two good daughters so I mustn't get miserable" she looked cheerful again.

Mother's sister Mary, (called Polly by Mother and Grandma) was often at Grandma's when we visited. The sisters were different in looks and temperament, although both were dark haired. Mary, a year or two younger than Mother, was a large lady who laughed a lot; while Mother was quite slim and serious. Tom, Mary's husband,

A Dot's Life by Dorothy Buchanan

was a slightly built man and much shorter in height than Mary. They lived in Timpron Street, near Smithdown Road, in the same area as Grandma.

Tom worked as a linesman for the railway. Their home was his pride and joy. In fact he kept it gleaming. Each time we visited he would either be doing household jobs or decorating. Mother took great delight in teasing Mary about Tom's interest in housework.

"I've never heard of a man wanting to do women's work," she'd say. "It's very odd."

In private, she and Dad made fun of Tom's looks and Mary's size. I felt sorry for Aunty Mary. She never seemed able to respond to Mothers taunting remarks.
Grandma told me they'd had a daughter a few months before I was born called Marjorie, but she had died while still a toddler. She said Aunty Mary never recovered the loss. It must have been very distressing for them both to see me constantly, knowing their child would have been a similar age.

"Your Mother and Polly never got on, you know," Grandma said as if reading my thoughts. "Your Mother had a privileged life being in service. She became a maid to a rich family in Mossley Hill. They employed a cook as well." (Mossley Hill was a posh area in the suburbs). Then, looking thoughtful, she added, "She even went on holidays with them and got a taste for the good life. Most Sundays she'd come home for a visit. I was always pleased to see her, but I dreaded the fuss she made. So full of airs and graces she was too. She lectured Polly and I on being more tidy and the correct way to do our housework. She was critical of everything"

"Why didn't you tell her off Grandma? I asked.

"She never bothered me. It all went in one ear and out the other. But it did upset our Polly a lot, I must admit."

I hadn't heard any of these stories before, but I knew Mother never encouraged Aunty Mary or Uncle Tom to visit us. Sometimes Aunty Mary would say, "We'll call and see you in the week, Maud," But Mother was always quick to reply;

"I'm far too busy this week. You can come some other

A Dot's Life by Dorothy Buchanan

time." But that "other time" never came. The only visits they made to our house were at Christmas time. Grandma banged the remains of the tobacco from the pipe into the fire. It had gone out.

"You can't get a decent smoke out of a pipe. You have to keep lighting the damn thing up." Then again reaching in her apron pocket she produced a packet of five Woodbine cigarettes. This was an eye opener. I felt I'd never really known her. I'd never seen her smoke when I visited her with Mother. I pretended not to notice, and looked into the fire.

"Do you want me to do any jobs Grandma?" I asked, as she blew clouds of smoke over my head.

"No, there's nothing to do. I'm not like your Mother you know, she spends her life cleaning and tidying up." I was more than relieved. Then she leaned forward and with a mischievous grin said

"I'll bet you're dying to have a puff, aren't you?" She handed me her cigarette. I was flabbergasted, but tried not to show it. I held the cigarette awkwardly not knowing what to do.

"Go on have a quick drag," she said. I put the wet end to my mouth pretending to puff it. Bits of tobacco stuck to my lips. It was horrible. I gave it back to her as quickly as I could.

"By the way," she said, taking another puff. "Don't you ever tell your Mother I smoke will you?"

"No. Of course not," I said quickly and tried to sound convincing. I had no intention of telling Mother anyway.

"Because if ever you do, I'll tell her YOU smoke too." She threw her head back and roared with laughter.

Chapter Four
Grandma Phillips and the Clay Pipe

For the next few weeks I enjoyed going to Grandma's. She was always full of fun. I had to pretend to mother I did lots of jobs, but of course I didn't do any, most of the time was spent eating and talking. Grandma did the smoking and I had an occasional puff too!

She told me lots of stories especially about Granddad. Apparently he spent every evening in the local pub drinking with his friends.
"He's what's called an "outdoor angel" and an "indoor devil," she explained. Then with a knowing smile, she said "But I have my ways of dealing with Will Phillips. Do you know what I do?" I had no idea what she was going to tell me.
"Well, when he comes home drunk he always hangs his coat on the back of his chair and dozes off, then I go through his pockets and take a few bob and hide it in my potato bag. The next morning he always says he thought he had more money, but I say "Your drunken friends must have pinched it." She gave a wicked grin. "It works every time."

I found some of her stories hard to believe, but I enjoyed listening to them.
Mother often asked me what Grandma talked about, or if I had ever seen her smoke, obviously she suspected she did. I was always very careful with my replies. I realised how different they were. Grandma was happy and carefree with a house as untidy as she was - Mother being completely the reverse.

Grandma and Granddad Phillips had a very odd relationship. He worked as a casual labourer on Lord Derby's estate. He often brought home "Spoils" as he called them. Usually a variety of vegetables in a potato sack, which he carried home over his shoulder. Grandma loved to tease him about the contents, although she was glad of them.
"Oh, been robbing again have you?" she'd taunt. He'd glare at her.

A Dot's Life by Dorothy Buchanan

"They'd only be wasted if I hadn't taken them," he'd grunt. Grandma would give me a wink and whisper; "Believe that, and you'll believe anything!"
Sometimes she'd find a rabbit or a pigeon in the sack which he'd poached with his catapult. He'd expect Grandma to cook whatever he'd brought home for their supper after his visit from the pub. Otherwise there'd be trouble.

He was a heavily built man with watery blue eyes, and his thick moustache dominated his round face. His cheeks looked permanently pink and shiny. He had wisps of silver hair on his balding head and took great care brushing them into place before he went to the pub each night. This never failed to amuse Grandma. He had a deep gruff voice. I was sometimes shocked at the way he spoke to Grandma. He'd rant and rage if he mislaid anything; and he was cantankerous most of the time. When she spoke to him, he would grunt his replies. Worst of all, he called her "Woman" rather than her name. It didn't seem to upset her at all. She would make faces behind his back, and call him "A soft old bugger" to his face. I often feared for her safety.

He once bought himself a pair of reading glasses from Woolworths. Not many people could afford to go to Opticians. Grandma was pleased as she badly needed reading glasses too. She used them regularly when he was out.

One day while I was there, he sat reading the paper with his prized glasses, the next minute he flung them across the table in temper shouting;
"I can't read with these glasses any more, you've worn them out, woman. I told you not to use them!" Grandma went into peals of laughter and said to me;
"Now you know why I call him *a soft old bugger*." Granddad ignored her, and went out muttering to himself. Strangely enough, when he spoke to me or his beloved cat, his voice would always sound soft and tender.

Grandma looked far more fragile than she actually was. She was a rounded lady, not very tall with short straight, thin black hair. So

A Dot's Life by Dorothy Buchanan

thin, you could see her yellowing scalp peeping through and her weathered face was deeply lined. Her poor hands were twisted with rheumatism and they looked very painful. But she never complained. She wasn't at all interested in clothes. Most times we visited she'd have on the same faded blue dress and a sack cloth apron across her waist with a big front pocket. Mother did her best to encourage her to wear other clothes, sometimes becoming angry with her, but Grandma never changed. She was happy as she was.

One of the stories Grandma enjoyed telling frequently, was when she found a hare in the sack Granddad had brought home, which she'd skinned and roasted for their supper. Unknown to her, Grandad had organised a raffle for the hare that evening in the pub. He'd sold most of the draw tickets spending the money on rounds of drinks. She heard him singing that night long before he opened the front door.

"Come on in you drunken Bugger, your supper's ready," she'd shouted.
A well dressed man accompanied Grandad into the kitchen.
"Give this gentleman the hare, Woman" he slurred. "He's won it in the raffle!"
"It's just come out of the oven. He'll have to eat it with us if he wants it." She thought the situation was hilarious and laughed loudly. Granddad of course was livid, he cursed and sputtered and stumbled around the living room making all kinds of threats to Grandma but nothing could be done. Then the gentleman became angry, shouting; "Is this some sort of a joke, making a fool out of me like this? You haven't heard the last of this." He stormed out of the house, banging the door. Granddad continued ranting and raving long after the man had left, his face purple with rage. But Grandma just sat eating the roast hare, giggling quietly to herself.

After that episode he didn't speak to her for quite some time. It took him weeks, to pay back the draw ticket money too! Grandma loved relating this story and always laughed as she must have done that fateful night for Granddad.

Now that David was getting older, Mother was able to resume her regular visits to Grandma's. I no longer went on my own. I noticed how very differently Grandma behaved when Mother was around. I missed the fun and chats we used to have.

Chapter Five
Daisy and the Bridesmaid

Grandma Lawrence (Dad's Mother) never visited our house, even at Christmas. She'd never forgiven him for marrying Mother. She felt she'd come from a very Common family and thought Dad could have done far better for himself; she even refused to attend their wedding. Mother disliked her equally. They never visited or spoke to each other, *ever*. Dad often took me to visit her on Sunday afternoons. She lived in Adelaide Road, in the Edge Hill area of Liverpool. Granddad Lawrence had died long before I was born. Their eldest daughter, Milly and youngest son Leslie, were still at home unmarried.

Although Leslie was engaged, her other two sons (my father, Cyril and Reg') had married years ago. Milly, now in her early forties, had worked in a Greengrocer's since leaving school. She had inherited the shop when the owner died. It was a thriving business too.

Grandma Lawrence was an elegant lady; her white hair always neat and tidy and her clothes looked expensive and tasteful. She held herself very erect, which made her appear taller and she always smelt of lavender. Her home reflected her in such a lot of ways; highly polished mahogany furniture, ornate clocks, lots of delicate ornaments, floral covered chairs and sofas, thick rugs, paintings, gilt framed mirrors, and vases of fresh flowers in most rooms - even the bathroom!

Having tea there was an event; a starched white embroidered tablecloth with matching napkins adorned her big round table, bone china, silver cutlery, and a bowl of fresh flowers in the centre. The food always complimented the setting, dainty sandwiches without crusts, some filled with Salmon and Cucumber or Ham and Tomato. Lots of fancy cakes on a two-tiered cake stand, hot buttered home-made scones, trifle with fresh cream, biscuits cheese and fresh fruit. I *loved* all the luxury.

A Dot's Life by Dorothy Buchanan

Grandma Lawrence liked refinement in manners, dress and appearance. She could be very critical if things weren't to her liking. She corrected me on numerous occasions about my table manners.

"Sit up properly, don't slouch like that" or "Don't speak with your mouth full, it's rude!" Her favourite comment seemed to be "You'll never grow up to be a lady, if you behave like that!" Her reprimands never bothered me, I enjoyed the attention! After the meal I sometimes helped her dry the dishes. When on our own, she often made comments about the dress or shoes I was wearing. Her remarks suggested that Mother had no taste. Her pet hate was my name, "Dorothy" she'd say. "Whatever possessed your mother to give you a name like that? You should have had a more aristocratic name, like Cecelia or Caroline." I didn't like my name, but I didn't like her choice either!

She often told me about her family, who'd come from Ulverston and her sister Magdalene, who owned a boarding house in the Isle of Man, where she and Auntie Milly spent regular summer holidays. It seemed unbelievable to me. I wondered what it would be like to go away on a holiday.

On Sunday afternoons Aunty Milly would wait for me on the corner of the street. Mother wouldn't allow her to call to the house. Uncle Leslie and his fiancée, Daisy, were having tea with us this particular Sunday and the date for their wedding was planned. Grandma was in her element discussing the arrangements with Daisy. She was very excited.

Daisy epitomised all the things Grandma admired; she was refined, extremely attractive and smartly dressed. She worked as a fashion buyer in a big department store. A highly thought of job at the time. I liked her very much and thought she was quite beautiful. She knew I loved seeing pictures of film stars and kept her Movie magazines for me so I could cut them out for my collection. She allowed me to try on her hats and paint my nails with her colourless nail polish. I always looked forward to seeing her. I listened to the conversation intently while we were having our meal as Auntie Daisy and Grandma discussed the details of the wedding. Then Grandma put her hand on my arm and looked at me smiling warmly, "Dorothy" she said. "We have something to tell you. Aunty Daisy wants you to be her bridesmaid. Isn't that wonderful? You'll look so pretty too." I was so delighted I could hardly speak, I never thought I'd ever be a bridesmaid!

"Oh thank you," I gasped, going red with excitement. "That will be marvellous," I said. "But I haven't got a bridesmaids dress." I suddenly felt very disappointed. Much to my surprise they all laughed.

"You don't have to worry about that. Aunty Daisy will take you to her shop and buy you a lovely dress and you'll be able to keep it afterwards," Grandma said looking admiringly at Daisy. I was bursting with happiness, I wanted to go home right away and tell mother the wonderful news.

"We're hoping to get married where your Dad works. It's such a lovely church, but that has to be arranged yet," Aunty Daisy told me.

All the way home I visualised myself in a lovely bridesmaids dress walking down the aisle behind Aunty Daisy with the organ playing. The same aisle I'd played along so many times. It was like a fairy tale!

As soon as Mother opened the front door I could hardly contain myself, jumping up and down hysterically shouting

"What do you think, I'm going to be a bridesmaid. Isn't it absolutely marvellous!"

"For heaven's sake calm down and tell me properly, whatever it is," Mother demanded. I tried to calm down but it was difficult. Eventually I sat down and told her in breathless bursts all the exciting news. There was a long pause. Mother didn't look pleased I couldn't understand why.

"So they think they are going to get married where your Father works do they?" She looked very annoyed. "What a blasted cheek." I ignored her remarks and carried on.

"They especially want me to be their bridesmaid. I'm so excited and what do you think, they said I could keep the dress afterwards!" Mother's expression didn't alter.

"You aren't going to be their bridesmaid and that's final." Her eyes flashed in anger. "They're not going to insult your Dad

A Dot's Life by Dorothy Buchanan

and me like this and get away with it!" She rasped, her face had now gone quite red. I was horrified. I couldn't believe what I was hearing.

"But it's all arranged," I shouted. "What do you mean, *insulting you*? They said they liked Dad's church, that's all." Tears of frustration and anger poured down my cheeks. "Anyway, whatever you say I AM going to be their bridesmaid and you can't stop me," I screeched. Just at that moment, Dad opened the front door and came into the living room.

"What's all the noise about?" He looked startled. I ran to him and poured out my story before he'd even taken his coat off. He didn't say anything. Instead he looked at Mother questioningly and waited for her response.

"If your Leslie thinks you're going to be a skivvy for him on his wedding day-" she was shouting now. "-He's got another think coming!" Her face twisted in anger. Dad looked worried.

"Calm down love. Let's have our tea and talk about it later. Maybe they didn't think of it that way?" he said soothingly. But Mother carried on

"And as for our Dorothy being their bridesmaid, well that's out of the question!" I felt I hated her, and I appealed to Dad.

"Tell her. I *am* going to be their bridesmaid. Aren't I?" He shuffled from one foot to the other, looking very uncomfortable.

"Stop crying now love," he said, patting my head. "Tears aren't going to solve anything. We'll just have to wait and see how things work out." I couldn't understand what things had to be sorted out? Mother refused to discuss the matter any further, in spite of my tears and pleadings.

I was bitterly upset. Mother said I was making such a song and dance about it and sent me to bed. I cried myself to sleep, while a fierce row was taking place downstairs.

Mother met me coming down the stairs the following morning.

"Your Dad and I have talked things over and you won't be going to any wedding; neither will we. And I don't want to hear another word about it. Is that clear?" She pushed her face close to mine. I couldn't bear to look at her. She sounded triumphant.

35

A Dot's Life by Dorothy Buchanan

The wedding didn't take place at Dad's church and I wasn't allowed to be a bridesmaid. It took me ages to get over the sadness I felt. I resented Mother and I was disappointed with Dad. Grandma Lawrence was livid and called Mother all kinds of names. She was angry with Dad too, saying;

"He lets that awful woman rule him." I understood how she felt and agreed with her. Aunty Daisy was very upset, saying *she never dreamt the choice of church would have caused such a lot of unpleasantness.* I expect she was equally annoyed with Mother and Dad, but she didn't voice her opinions in front of me. She just said she was disappointed I wasn't able to be her bridesmaid. Which made me feel worse!

I don't know where the wedding took place, but I was given a piece of wedding cake in a silver box and shown the photographs by Aunty Daisy. I treasured the cake and looked at it often without ever eating it. They bought a house in the same road as Grandma Lawrence, so each time I visited Grandma I called to see them too.

I was always delighted with the presents I received for Christmas and Birthdays from Grandma Lawrence, Aunty Milly and Daisy. They never asked me what I wanted, as Mother and Grandma Phillips did, but I was never disappointed; silver bracelets, necklaces, rabbit wool gloves and a matching scarf, an umbrella, books, all sorts of lovely surprises. They would be wrapped with pretty paper and tied with ribbon and a card attached would have my name neatly written.

Mother and Grandma Phillips always asked me weeks before what I would like for birthdays or Christmas, then give me whatever I'd chosen unwrapped on the day. Somehow I'd lost interest by then and usually felt disappointed.

A Dot's Life by Dorothy Buchanan

Chapter Six
Clean Up and Tea Time

During the long summer break from school, no children in our street went away on holidays, but we'd plan lots of things to do. None of us were ever given any pocket money, but we became quite inventive. We'd call on neighbours' houses and ask if they had any empty jam jars; the grocers paid us a penny for a two pound jar and a halfpenny for a one pound jar. If this failed we would clean front steps on our hands and knees with a bucket of water a scrubbing brush and a lump of sandstone, which the lady of the house would provide. For this chore we would get three pence.

Sometimes we'd run errands too. Some of the girls used to help their Mothers in the morning to "clean up" as it was called. This entailed beating the mats over a clothes line in the back yard, washing the floors with a mop and bucket and dusting the furniture. If I called for one of them when this was taking place, their Mother's would say,
"Come on in you're just in time to give your pal a hand."
I loved getting involved. It made me feel like one of the family - we would be rewarded with three-pence each too! I asked Mother if I could "clean up" for her.
She looked amazed;
"Clean up for me! No thank you, unlike the Mothers around here I do my own housework properly."
"But lots of my friends' Mothers let them do it for them, and they pay them too."
"Oh, so its money you're after is it, not helping me at all," she sneered. I found her difficult to understand sometimes.

The money we collected during the week with our numerous ventures meant we could go to the pictures on Saturday afternoon, buy sweets and have an ice cream, which was a great treat. We would all make our way in high spirits to the Hope Hall cinema (commonly called the Flea Pit) which was just around the corner from Myrtle Street Baptist church were Dad worked.

A Dot's Life by Dorothy Buchanan

The cinema is now the famous "Everyman Theatre" in Hope Street, Liverpool.
We'd arrive early and queue outside, everyone screaming and shouting, in anticipation. Once the doors opened it was like a stampede getting to the box office to buy our tickets.

Saturday was the only day children were allowed in without an adult and once inside everyone tried to get front seats, believing them to be the best, although we usually came out with stiff necks! Most of the seats were broken. Some had springs sticking out, and the floor was bare boards, but it didn't matter to us.

There was always a lot of pushing and shoving going on and the cinema employed attendants to keep order. They walked up and down the aisles with long sticks and poked children, who misbehaved. The stick was used quite a lot.

Before the lights went out disinfectant was sprayed down each aisle from a long metal cylinder with a pump. It was called "Flit." We covered our faces when he got near to us, but we still smelt of it for the rest of the day. Once the film began we all cheered. It was usually a Cowboy film, and everyone got involved in the story; when the "Baddie" came on we booed loudly. When he was hurt or killed we'd cheer and shout "Hooray."

Quite often the film would break down, sometimes at an exciting moment and then the noise became deafening with stamping feet, shouting and chanting "Why are we waiting." Once it came on again everyone cheered. Sometimes the cheering went on so long we'd miss some of the film. Two films were always shown, a full length one, and a serial. The serial was usually the most exciting, but just at a tense moment big letters would cover the screen saying, "DON'T MISS NEXT WEEKS' THRILLING INSTALMENT." That was always disappointing as we could never go every week!

Mother never knew I went to the Hope Hall with all the local children. I knew if I'd asked her she would have refused to let me go to such a place. I always told her I was going to play with June

A Dot's Life by Dorothy Buchanan

Furlong for the afternoon. She approved of June, probably because she lived in a well kept house and she was always neat and tidy. June spent most of her time playing indoors with her abundance of toys and games. I did go to her house occasionally, but not as many times as mother thought. Mother didn't approve of any of the children in our street, she found fault with all of them. If they called for me to play out, she treated them with contempt.

"I have more to do with my time than answer the door to you, now run away and play," she'd say. Consequently not many called. Her attitude upset me.
I was always made so welcome at their houses and usually asked inside. I tried to explain to Mother how nice their parents were to me when I called at their houses.

"I don't want to encourage those sort of children here, and I'm far too busy to be answering the door all the time," was her usual reply.

"Why can't I ask Jean into our house sometime, because she's my best friend?" I asked one day, and to my surprise she said "I WILL let you invite her, one day."

"But *when*," I shouted.

"Don't raise your voice to me. She'll be invited when it's convenient to me, and not before," she shouted back. I knew better than to pursue it any further but I was pleased, nevertheless. A few weeks later, Mother surprised me by saying I could ask Jean to have tea with me the following day. I was more than delighted. I never dreamt Mother would allow her come to tea! When I told Jean she didn't answer right away, but looked bemused.

"Tea, in your house? You're kidding me, aren't you?" she grinned.

"No. Of course I'm not," I said, feeling pleased with myself.

"Your Mother won't expect me to get dressed up will she?"

"No. Don't be daft," I said. But her remark made me think. I'd never really noticed what Jean looked like or what she wore. But I knew Mother would notice everything. I took a side long look at her, with Mothers' eyes. A thin pale faced girl, with a thick mop of unruly brown hair, clothes that seemed far too big for her, a large safety pin holding up her skirt, a crumpled dull white

A Dot's Life by Dorothy Buchanan

blouse with buttons missing - and she had a grey tide mark around her face. Mother would certainly notice all these things! I just hoped and prayed she would wear something else and give herself a bit more of a wash. I didn't want Mother to make any nasty remarks about her, but I didn't voice any of my fears to Jean. I was frightened of putting her off coming.

In spite of this worry I was happy. At last one of my friends was at last coming to our house, for tea as well, that was more than I'd hoped for. Afterwards, I could show Jean my bedroom and my collection of film star pictures she'd like them, we could play a few games too. I began to plan the evening carefully I was looking forward to it, so much. I just hoped Mother wouldn't make too much fuss, or ask Jean a lot of questions.

Jean arrived at five o'clock - the time Mother suggested. She'd obviously gone to a lot of trouble. She looked clean; an aroma of carbolic soap wafted from her, even her clothes looked pressed. Her hair looked more controlled too. I was pleased and relieved. Everything was going to be fine, I was delighted.

"Come on in Jean, don't forget to wipe your feet," Mother shouted from the living room. Jean did as she was asked for much longer than needed. I noticed the table was set for three. I was hoping we could have had tea on our own. But still, Mother did seem to be in a good mood, although I knew Jean would feel uncomfortable sitting at the table with her. She stood awkwardly in the hall.
"Hello Mrs Lawrence," she shouted, taking off her coat and hanging it on the hallstand.
"How is the baby?" She continued. "Can I see him?" I knew she was doing her best to please Mother.
Mother was taken aback. "He's very well, thank you, but it's not convenient to see him just now. He's asleep in the other room and I don't want him disturbed." Jean looked puzzled, most people she knew loved showing their babies off to everyone.
I wished she hadn't asked about seeing David. It wasn't a good start.

A Dot's Life by Dorothy Buchanan

"Well come along in, and sit at the table," Mother held out a chair for her.

I sat by her, Mother opposite. I was disappointed when I saw the table. It looked very elaborate with diamond cut meat paste sandwiches and jam butties on doyleys, the best china tea set was being used too, the cutlery was gleaming. I knew Jean would feel out of place in this setting. If only Mother wasn't there observing us too!

While she poured the tea I passed Jean the sandwiches.

"Where does your Father work Jean?" Mother enquired.

"He's a Docker - and when he's not working he's in the pub. Mam says it's a good job he's in work otherwise he'd be in the pub all day!" Jean thought this funny and giggled. Mother wasn't amused and ignored the remark.

"Which school do you go to?" she began further questioning.

"I go to Granby Street it's a bit rough but I can take care of myself, I can give as good as I get!" Mother wasn't as impressed as Jean thought she'd be.

"Dorothy goes to St. Margaret's school. There aren't any ruffians there. They wouldn't tolerate behaviour like that," Mother said haughtily. I was cringing now. Jean didn't know how to reply, she was looking as uncomfortable as I felt.

Mother watched her every move. I tried my best to keep a light conversation going but it was useless, Mother insisted on further questions. Jean was stumbling with replies now. The meal progressed tensely. I kept wishing Mother would shut up. Jean and I hadn't been able to talk to each other at all.

I just wanted the meal to finish quickly so we could be on our own and I could show her all my film star pictures and games. Then an awful moment occurred; Jean dropped her jam buttie on the floor. She was nervous and her face went bright red. She bent down picked it up and was just about to put it in her mouth when Mother shouted in a horrified tone.

"Oh no, you mustn't eat anything that's been on the floor! Surely you know that!" Jean didn't know what to say or do, especially with the jam buttie. She put it on her plate then on the edge of the table, then back on her plate, as Mother shook her head

A Dot's Life by Dorothy Buchanan

and sighed disapprovingly.

"It's alright Jean, just leave it there," I whispered. She looked flustered and didn't appear to hear me, then stood up looking very embarrassed.

"Oh I've just remembered I have to go. I've got to mind me sister's baby. Thanks for the tea." She gushed the words out in one breath, ran from the table grabbing her coat from the hall stand and was out through the front door in a flash. I got up to follow her. I knew she was upset - so was I; but Mother pushed me back in my chair.

"Just you sit down and finish your tea. That girl has no manners, running out like that, whatever the reason. I've never seen such behaviour!"

"It was your fault she did that," I was close to tears. "You made her feel embarrassed - staring at her and asking her questions all the time!"

"How dare you speak to me like that; After me going out of my way to make you both a lovely tea. Why should she mind a few questions if she has nothing to hide?" Mother said nastily. Then she began raising her voice "It's obvious she's dragged up like the rest of them around here, with a Father getting drunk all the time." I quickly finished my tea and ran to my bedroom, I didn't want to hear any more but she carried on shouting to me up the stairs.

"We don't live like *those* people, and I don't want you *mixing with them* either. Is that understood?" I put the pillow over my head trying not to hear. Why did Mother behave like this? I'd never understand her.

Much later I made my way downstairs, dreading the reception I was going to get, but Mother was busy in the kitchen the table had been cleared as if the event had never happened!

"You can help David get ready for bed," she shouted. "Then go up to bed yourself!" She was still in the kitchen when I went up, but nothing more was said. I was thankful at least for that and went to bed feeling very miserable. It took me a long time to get to sleep. I kept wondering what Jean must think of Mother and what I was going to say to her? I had hoped so much for a lovely evening.

A Dot's Life by Dorothy Buchanan

The following day I called to Jean's house, (Mother didn't know of course) I was never going to stop seeing her, whatever she said. As I waited for a reply I suddenly thought, *perhaps Jean wouldn't want to see me again?* I hadn't thought of that until now. I kept thinking of what I should say to her, but nothing seemed right. The door opened. Jean stood there with a sheepish grin.

"Hi Dot, come on in, I won't be long. By the way I'm sorry I had to go home early last night, but I'd forgotten I had to mind our Sheila's baby honest." I was so relieved.

"It's alright I know you did," I said, knowing this lie resolved the situation for both of us.

"Hey, your Mother's a right snob though, isn't she?" Jean began mimicking Mother. I laughed at her attempts then joined in the fun with her. Everything was alright again, I was relieved and happy.

Chapter Seven
We Interrupt this Programme...

David was now a toddler. I still didn't bother with him much, but I had to take him walks and visit Grandma Lawrence and Aunty Milly each Sunday. Dad hardly ever went now. Hhe was too busy with church duties. Aunty Milly waited on the corner of the street for us as Mother had instructed. She still wasn't allowed to call at the house. I used to look out of the parlour window for her. When she arrived, I'd call to Mother -

"Aunty Milly's there. We're going now."

"You will go when I tell you and not before," was Mother's reply. She enjoyed making Aunty Milly wait, even in the rain. David and I always had a good time with Aunty Milly; she took us on tram rides and allowed us to sit upstairs in the front seats - something Mother or Dad would never agree to.

She took us to lots of places, one of our favourites being Sefton Park, which held a lot of interest for us. We'd walk to the aviary to see the birds, go on a rowing boat on the big lake, then sit on a seat eating sweets in the Palm House surveying all the exotic flowers and plants and white marble statues. Finally we'd go to the bronze Peter Pan statue and trace out the tiny hidden animals with our fingers. Occasionally, we'd go to Woolton woods or a walk through Allerton cemetery. We would read names on tomb stones, and collect Crab Apples that seemed to grow in abundance.

We often went to the Pier Head and took the ferry across the Mersey. She explored the boat with us and once even asked the Captain if we could have a look in the engine room which we did, and that was really exciting. She appeared to enjoy everything as much as we did, after our afternoon trips we'd go back to her house for our lovely tea. Sometimes, after tea Aunty Milly would bring out a box of "Black Magic" chocolates. I thought they were wonderful. She let us choose the centres of our choice too. When all the chocolates were eaten she'd let me take the box home. I treasured that black shiny box with its red tassels, and kept it in my bedroom.

A Dot's Life by Dorothy Buchanan

Each time I opened it I could smell the sweet smell of chocolate!

After tea Grandma usually listened to her favourite Brass Band music on the wireless and she'd encourage David and I to march around the room like soldiers while she clapped her hands in time to the music.

It was during one of these afternoons that the programme was interrupted with an important announcement. *War had been declared on Germany.* Grandma and Aunty Milly became very upset. I couldn't understand how war with Germany could possibly affect us? We were taken home very quickly. Mother looked very worried when we arrived home.

"It's terrible news. We're at war with Germany and all the men will be called up in the forces to fight the Germans!" I hadn't thought of that.

"Will Dad have to go and fight too?" I asked. "No he's too old. They only take the younger men, thank goodness." She looked relieved with this thought.

Everyone seemed to be talking about the war. Our street was full of people clustered in groups, saying *bombs might be dropped on us any minute!* The news bulletins on the wireless were listened to by everyone regularly. Most people began preparing for air raids, they glued brown paper strips across their window panes to protect them from shattering glass and some made a decorative feature out of this with diamond or cross designs.

No house or building could show any light from outside, so blackout curtains had to be put up at every window. Black paint was used to obliterate the name "LIVERPOOL" from everything; road signs, trams, lorries, railway stations and posters. The street lights on main roads were muted and most side streets had none at all.

Gas Masks were issued to everyone - adults being issued with them in a cardboard box holder with a long leather strap to carry across your shoulder, young children had Mickey Mouse masks which were made of blue rubber with a floppy red nose and silver eyelets. David had one of these.

A Dot's Life by Dorothy Buchanan

Mothers with young babies were given huge rubber cylinders to place the baby, with an outside pump to give the baby constant oxygen and a broad viewing area. Fortunately no gas masks were ever required, except for practice (but at the time we all thought they would be).

Lots of men got their calling up papers to join the forces as Mother predicted, and some joined up of their own accord especially if they were unemployed.
Uncle Leslie was called up, and went into the Royal Air Force. Grandma Lawrence, Daisy and Aunty Milly were devastated. Lots of families in our street had noisy parties the night before their husbands or sons went off to war. The following morning they would be crying on the steps waving them goodbye.

Air Raid Sirens were practised daily now. A very loud up and down sound for an on-coming "Air Raid" and a long one note sound for the "All Clear." The noise was so deafening you could hear it everywhere. Big silver barrage balloons went up high in the sky. Presumably, they would ignite if a plane touched them.
Emergency water tanks were erected in lots of open spaces E.W.S painted on the side. Some daring boys used to swim in them!

Air Raid wardens were recruited, mostly middle aged men. They were given tin hats with ARP written on the front. Their job was to help and instruct people during an air raid, making sure people were safe, that no lights were visible from outside houses etc.

Male family members began reinforcing cellars or under stairways, with planks of wood that lined the walls and ceiling for safety during any bombing. Dad did this to the bottom of our cellar stairs. He even erected a small shelf to hold a candle, matches and a bell, in case we were ever trapped.

The war and the preparations for the bombing were talked about by everyone constantly. At school we had air raid practices regularly, we had to go to an air raid shelter in the cellar of a building opposite our school. It was all very exciting to us, especially

A Dot's Life by Dorothy Buchanan

climbing the ladder to get in the cellar.

Big lorries came into our street one day to collect any iron we had. Lots of people gave them flat irons, pokers and steel kettles, then much to everyone's amazement they began uprooting the railings and gates from the fronts of the houses! All the householders were out shouting and swearing at the men for removing them, but they carried on saying "Sorry Misses, but we have our orders; it's for the War Effort." Dad spent a lot of his spare time replacing the iron railing with a wooden fence, much to Mothers relief but not many other people bothered.

Public Air Raid shelters made of concrete and reinforced with steel girders began to be built in lots of side streets. One was erected in front of our house! Mother of course was livid, but there was nothing she could do except complain; which she did daily.

At the back of our house (in Huskisson Street, where Beryl Bainbridge once lived – number 12) stood a large empty building that was once a Domestic Science college. The vast cellars were now being reinforced to make a public air raid shelter, which would hold quite a number of people. Jean and I watched as lots of heavy planks of wood, steel girders, chairs and benches were taken in.

The first time the sirens went off was in the early evening, we had just finished tea. Mother and Dad were in a panic. Dad rushed upstairs and brought down a holdall. Mother ran around switching off lights and gas.

"Hurry up into the cellar," shouted Dad. "This is an air raid alright." He looked very worried. Mother carried David down into the cellar. Dad carried the bag, pushing me ahead of him. We all sat on the stairs feeling very frightened, huddled together in candle light. Everywhere was quiet. After about half an hour the All Clear sounded.

"It must have been a false alarm," Dad said, looking relieved. As we made our way upstairs I wondered why Dad had taken the bag with him.

"Why did you take that bag Dad? What's in it?" I enquired.
"Inside here are all our worldly goods," he said smiling.

"If an air raid occurs when I'm not in, I'm relying on you to take this in the cellar for me."

"What are worldly goods?" I was intrigued.

"Insurance policies, your mothers watch, engagement ring, the rent book, and any money that we have."

I don't know what I expected but I was disappointed.

Further raids followed, but they were like the first. We became accustomed to nothing happening and it got very boring sitting for ages on the cellar stairs. We heard lots of reports on the wireless of dreadful raids and people being killed in other parts of the country, mostly in London and South coast areas.

Chapter Eight
The Shelters in the Cellar and the College

One night, after the siren had sounded, we sat as usual on the cellar stairs. For the first time since the raids began we heard the drone of heavy aircraft overhead. This was unusual we'd never heard them before.

"They'll be our planes searching for any German bombers," Dad had hardly finished his sentence, when a loud bang like a heavy clap of thunder sounded somewhere near! Mother and I screamed with shock. David began crying loudly. Dad was doing his best to calm us.

"It's alright, it's alright keep calm all of you," he shouted. At that moment a terrific explosion sounded and within seconds Dads reinforced alcove shook and collapsed around us missing David and I by inches! Mother became hysterical screaming at Dad-

"We're all going to be killed. Do something Cyril, for God's sake!" Dad did his best to comfort her while trying to hold up the planks of wood. He kept telling us to go upstairs but we all seemed rooted to the spot. Then he lost control.

"Just get up the bloody stairs right away will you, I can't hold on to this lot much longer!" He screamed. I'd never heard him shout or swear at Mother before, or look so angry. His face was red and big blue veins stuck out on his forehead. Without another word, we all ran up the stairs and under the dining room table until the All Clear sounded. We were all very shocked and frightened.

Outside seemed quiet now. Dad was giving Mother Aspirins and cups of tea to calm her, and David was still crying. I was shaking like a leaf.

"That was a near miss. I thought we'd all be killed. I wonder where that bomb dropped? It was definitely not far from here," Mother said between sobs. It took a long time for her to compose herself.

"Next time there's an air raid," she said. "We'll be going to that shelter in the Domestic Science College. I'm not chancing

A Dot's Life by Dorothy Buchanan

staying here any longer!"

The college, with its vast cellars now reinforced professionally, was a better alternative to our make-shift arrangement. Nobody ever thought of using the concrete shelters that had been built in the front street, they were used as toilets by drunks coming home from the pub and reeked of urine. I was secretly hoping for an Air Raid, so I could see what it was like inside the college shelter.

The next raid came the following night, quicker than anyone anticipated! Mother and Dad, David and I all rushed into the entry and through the back gate of the college to the door of the shelter. Searchlights were scanning the sky. Lots of people were already there shouting, swearing and getting abusive with the Air Raid Warden, who was standing guard at the entrance. He was trying to make himself heard above all the noise.

"For Christ's sake will you all be quiet and listen. I can only let four of you in at a time, otherwise the light will be seen outside!" Not many heard him, they were shouting and screaming and trying to push their way through the door. I was jostled around by the angry crowd and no longer with Mother and Dad, I called them but my voice was drowned with the din I tried my best to find them but it was hopeless being so dark too. Eventually I was pushed through the heavy door with three strangers into a small passage (the heavy iron door closing behind us then a further door opened into the glaring lights of the shelter). Not seeing Mother and Dad, I realised they still hadn't yet got in. After a few minutes Mother appeared looking very angry and, seeing me, shouted-

"Why didn't you keep with us: we could have been killed looking for you. You damned nuisance! Keep with us in future, do you hear!" She pushed passed me into the corridor before I could explain. I followed her, feeling humiliated, knowing everyone must have heard her shouting at me. The long corridor was full, I'd never seen so many people, some sitting on benches against the walls, others making a bed for themselves with blankets on the floor, some were unpacking bags with flasks of tea, and sandwiches. Lots were singing and laughing very loudly. The air was a haze of cigarette smoke.

A Dot's Life by Dorothy Buchanan

The walls had been whitewashed and the floors were concrete. The numerous iron girders were everywhere, securing the ceilings. Two rooms off the corridor housed lots more people on benches. "We'll sit in here," Mother decided, making her way into the first room and claiming three seats. Nobody was lying on the floor in here, or singing, everyone seemed to be quietly talking in hushed tones. In the distance rumbling could be heard, more like thunder than bombs or gunfire. But it felt safe in the shelter. I was getting bored just sitting staring ahead of me, listening to the fun that seemed to be going on in other parts of the shelter. I was anxious to go and explore and see if any of my friends were around, but I didn't dare ask, knowing Mother was still angry with me. David became restless sitting on Mothers knee. This was my chance.

"Can I take David for a walk around?"

"Yes, that's a good idea, but watch him carefully won't you" I assured her I would. I was in my element exploring everywhere with David. There must have been a few hundred people there! Some young fellows and girls at the far end of the shelter were all singing and I could hear a guitar being played. As I made my way towards them dragging David along, I spotted Jean amongst the crowd.

"Hi Dot" she grinned, looking pleased to see us.

"Come over here, I'm glad you're come to this shelter"

"Look, our Jimmy's brought his Guitar, and he can't half play too, listen" She looked admiringly at her brother.

"I'll lift your David up so he can see." With that she hauled him over her shoulder. I just hoped Mother wouldn't come looking for us. A big crowd had gathered around Jimmy as he stood playing. I'd never seen anyone play a guitar before, it was all very thrilling. I thought Jimmy was wonderful. He was very handsome. All the girls were pushing each other to get closer to him. Then they all began singing. Jean and I joined in, although we didn't know the words to any of the popular songs (like most of the older girls and boys) but it didn't matter. We sang just the same and enjoyed ourselves. I hoped it would go on all night! Much to my disappointment, after about an hour the all clear sounded. I quickly made my way back to Mother and Dad.

"Where did you get to? I was getting worried," said Mother, while David was repeating "I saw the band! I saw the

A Dot's Life by Dorothy Buchanan

band!"
"That would be the music he heard," Mother said. I made no comment. I couldn't wait to go to the shelter again!

The raids became more frequent - so lot's of visits were made. Quite quickly everyone got to know everyone else and claimed their particular spot. Some had seats, some occupied the floor and others stood in groups around the doorway.
One man stood out from the rest; he was dressed very smartly whatever time the raid began. He stood alone and didn't talk to anyone, although he always made a big fuss of David each time he saw him, lifting him up and giving him a hug. The shelter folk made unkind remarks about him between themselves and referred to him as the "Mystery Man".
"He must go to bed dressed like that," they'd say and laugh. One evening, during a raid, a policeman and two plain clothes men came into the shelter. They wandered around for awhile much to everyone's curiosity. Then they surrounded the Mystery Man. A crowd gathered around him wondering what was going on, but after a brief chat the policeman handcuffed the man and led him outside. There was a buzz of excitement everyone had their own theories as to who he was or what he had done. Most decided he was a German spy. Whoever he was or whatever happened to him we never found out.

A year or so later, a parcel arrived at our house addressed to "David" of Egerton Street, Liverpool. The wrapping was badly torn and the post mark unreadable. We never received parcels and Mother was very apprehensive about opening it, but David and I were anxious to find out what it could be. When finally the last paper was removed, there sat a very expensive looking sailing boat with "David" painted in neat little letters on the side. David was thrilled and even took it to bed with him that night. There was no message or address in the parcel, just the boat. I felt sure the Mystery Man had sent it, but we would never know, it was a lovely gift nevertheless. David treasured it for years.
A scheme was brought out to evacuate children from inner city schools to country places to avoid the bombing. From Liverpool, most of the children would be sent to Wales. The schools had the

A Dot's Life by Dorothy Buchanan

job of organising it. Living in the country sounded exciting and I badly wanted to go. Mother and Dad weren't keen on the idea but agreed reluctantly to let me go. I was so pleased as lots of my friends were going and we talked about it endlessly, thinking it would be like a long holiday. The day arrived for my departure. My little leather case was packed and a luggage label with my name and school, attached to my lapel. We didn't know who we'd be living with until we arrived. Just before I was about to leave the house, Mother began to cry

"It's no use I can't let you go," she sobbed. I became very angry and ranted on for ages, but I knew I wouldn't be going. As it happened, lots of children who did go, were very unhappy with their placements and returned home quite quickly. Only two girls I knew were settled in good homes and stayed in Wales for the duration of the war.

After that first scramble to get into the shelter, everyone now behaved more orderly. We usually saw the searchlights scanning the sky while we waited our turn to go in, and for some reason they gave us a secure feeling. I looked forward to seeing my friends too, especially Jean, she hadn't been evacuated either. We played cards or sang songs and often stood with the older fellows and girls listening to their conversations. We'd pull faces at each other when we heard them swear but they all made quite a fuss of us. It was hard to believe an Air Raid was going on outside, except when we heard gunfire and then everyone would cheer loudly.

As lots of young men had been called up, there were vacancies in jobs for older men, and Dad managed to get a job in Bibby's, a Cattle food manufacturer. It was far better paid than being a caretaker of a church; the only problem being shift work (early mornings, afternoons and nights, rotating each week). Mother hated being on her own at night.

It was now May 1941. School work had altered a lot. With the threat of pending air raids we concentrated on Reading, Writing and Arithmetic not much Art, Science, History or Geography. I enjoyed reading very much and we read out loud in class from famous books like "The Black Arrow," but I hated Arithmetic - probably because I wasn't very good at it! We didn't have any exams or homework so our evenings were free.

About four o'clock one morning the sirens sounded and we all dragged ourselves from sleep and rushed to the air raid shelter. Once inside, the tiredness disappeared. As usual the atmosphere was noisy with lots of chatter and laughter and some folks already singing! I always felt happy and secure there. As usual I quickly wandered off to find Jean. The older girls and fellows were having a guessing game and allowed us to join in. We loved being involved with them, although we were both only eleven. They made us feel grown up!

A lot of noise was going on outside, but it was no different than we'd heard many times before. We could hear the drone of heavy planes overhead and a lot of gunfire. Everyone was settling down to their various pursuits and then quite unexpectedly a deafening bang occurred. The building shook. Those standing were thrown to the floor - the force was unbelievable! I felt terrified as I was also thrown to the floor. I thought at any moment, the building would collapse on top of us.

The noise of the raid outside could still be heard in spite of the screaming and shouting in the shelter. Guns were still firing and heavy planes were overhead with many more explosions. Some people in the shelter were hurt when they were thrown to the ground. Although I ended up on the floor I wasn't hurt. I slowly stood up, but I was shaking uncontrollably. I watched the warden doing his best to get some order out of the chaos and help the injured. Panic had set in and a body of people were banging their fists on the front door. "We'll all be killed in here you've got to let us out," they screamed at the warden. Babies everywhere were crying. Complete mayhem seem to take over. The warden was frantic trying to tell everyone to lie on the floor for safety but not many heeded his advice, most were too hysterical. I wasn't able to get to the room were Mother Dad and David were, I tried to push through the crowds, but it was hopeless, I didn't know what I should do. After what seemed like hours the All Clear eventually sounded. I was as relieved to see Mother, Dad and David, as they

A Dot's Life by Dorothy Buchanan

were to see me.

Once in the street, dawn was breaking and the smell of phosphorus was very strong. The sky was alight with reflective fires and we arrived home to find the back door wide open, blown open by a blast, the living room window rested on the dining room table as if it had been placed there- the window panes intact! Thick dust was everywhere and as Dad ran up the stairs to see if we had any further damage, I followed. There was a strong smell of burning in the house, he inspected every room. When we got to the front bedroom he pushed me out saying

"Get me the bin lid and the shovel quick!" I took them up as fast as I could. Mother was distraught she shouted up the stairs to Dad-

"What's the matter Cyril what's burning? I can't stand much more of this!" But Dad and I ignored her. When I entered the room Dad was inspecting a long thick silver object on the floor, in front of the fireplace.

"Keep well back. This is a bomb and it hasn't gone off properly. It's burnt all the linoleum and look at that hole in the ceiling!" He pointed with a trembling hand to a gaping hole where the flaming sky was peeping through! I was far more interested in the bomb and I viewed it from all angles - a long silver cylinder with part of the end burnt. I was fascinated to think that bomb had been brought all the way from Germany just to land on our house! My previous fear in the shelter vanished. This was a big status symbol and I could hardly wait to tell my friends. I felt almost proud. Dad very carefully placed the bomb on the shovel and covered it quickly with the bin lid, then ceremoniously carried it slowly down the stairs and into the backyard. Dad spent a long time cleaning away the thick dust and fixing the window back in place. Repairing the hole in the ceiling proved more difficult as he only had bits of linoleum and wood to cover it.

The following morning Dad put the bomb in the rubbish bin and in the afternoon the bin was emptied. I watched as the bin men threw the contents into the Dust Cart, unaware of the bomb!

The big explosion we'd experienced that previous night was a Land

A Dot's Life by Dorothy Buchanan

Mine that was dropped on a large house in Parliament Street, a main road which I crossed each day going to school. The house was completely demolished. It was just a mountain of rubble. Rescue workers with tin hats and hankies over their mouths were already digging in the mound of debris. A lot of people were believed to be in the house at the time and a big crowd had gathered, hoping to see someone rescued. Jean and I were amazed to see the damage the bomb had done to the adjoining houses.

Most houses had windows blown out and huge chunks of masonry missing. The street was littered with broken glass, gravel, and bricks - and here and there were pieces of glinting silver shrapnel. Lots of children were collecting it and boasting when they found a large piece.

Jean and I joined the crowd that had gathered to watch the men dig for survivors, there was a peculiar smell in the air. Gradually the hole they were digging became deeper and now each spade-full produced something different; fragments of chairs, tables, toys, clothing, and bedding. The crowd watched in silence except when these items appeared then they would say "Ooh!" in unison. One of the rescue workers spotted a slippered foot peeping out of the debris and called the other fellows to help him, they all dug furiously. The crowd swayed forward to get a better look, hoping to see someone rescued, more of the leg appeared as they gently eased away the debris, then to everyone's horror - that was all there was! The screams from the crowd were deafening for a moment. Then it went deadly quiet, everyone slowly walked away, crying at such a dreadful sight. Jean and I went home in silence. We were equally shocked. We didn't know any of the people who lived there, but they must have all been in the cellars sheltering when the house got a direct hit. There were no survivors from that house. We tried hard not to think about it, but throughout the next few days we relived that moment again and again. We were thankful we used the big shelter, believing that could not have been obliterated so easily.

The following evening the sirens sounded just as David and I were about to have our tea. Raids held far more fear now and we all dashed to get to the shelter as quickly as we could, settling ourselves

A Dot's Life by Dorothy Buchanan

down to what might be a long night ahead. David began crying asking for his tea and I was also very hungry.

"Are you SURE you haven't brought anything to eat with you?" I asked Mother for the umpteenth time. She was already irritated with David crying.

"I didn't have time to get anything. You know that. Stop asking ridiculous questions!" Then as an afterthought she said, "If you are so desperate for something to eat, go and ask the warden if he'll go with you to our house and get those scones I made this afternoon."

"But I might get killed!" I shouted. I was horrified at her suggestion.

"Don't be silly. The warden will know when it's safe to make a dash for it. You can run there and back in no time at all!" I was terribly hungry so was David. Mother and Dad had had their meal earlier, so they were alright. I felt frightened and a bit excited as I went to look for the warden. He didn't seem at all surprised at my request. Maybe a lot of other people had done the same?

"Just keep with me. We'll chance it when it gets a bit quieter," he said, as we waited by main iron door.

It was very dark when we got outside and waited in the doorway, but the sky was bright with searchlights. The sound of gunfire and explosions could be heard in the distance. We waited for awhile and then the warden took my hand.

"Come on. Let's make a run for it!" When we reached our back door after running across the entry he said-

"Go on. I'll wait here for you." I was shaking so much it took me awhile to find the keyhole. After a bit of fumbling at last the door opened. I could smell the aroma of baked scones but couldn't think where they would be. Stumbling around in the dark kitchen was frustrating as my hands seemed to touch unfamiliar objects. I was patting the same things over again and the sound of heavy planes now overhead, made me nervous. I'd never heard them so loudly before and I began to panic. At last I remembered where Mother would have put the scones, they would be in the cake tin on top of the food cabinet. I usually stood on a chair to reach it. I gave a few jumps and managed to dislodge it onto the floor. Fortunately it didn't burst open. I shook it to make sure the scones were inside, then tucked it under my arm quickly locking the back door after me, then, ran as fast as I could to find the warden.

The air was thick with horrible smelling smoke and the noise of explosions, planes and gunfire deafening, searchlights were still flashing overhead as I got to the entry. My heart was beating fast. I expected to find the warden waiting, but nobody seemed to be there! I was terrified as I ran towards the shelter, the sky seemed crowded now with planes flying low. One of them appeared to be swooping down towards me like a huge black eagle. I stood looking at it not knowing what to do. Then someone grabbed the back of my coat and pushed me face downwards to the ground.

"Quick lie down. Put your hands over your head," he shouted gruffly. I immediately did as he asked. He lay close beside me. The cake tin rolled somewhere across the ground as we heard repeated machine gun sounds all around. They were aiming at us! I was petrified by now. I thought we'd be killed any minute. I was so thankful I was with the warden. Then as quickly as it began it was over and the plane made off. It all seemed more like a nightmare! I felt myself being pulled to my feet, my legs were wobbling like jelly. I couldn't control them.

"Come on let's get in that shelter before any more"Jerries" think we're sitting targets!"

"I have to find the cake tin first," I gasped.

"Never mind that now," he sounded angry. Just at that moment my foot kicked it. I picked it up as quickly as I could, thankfully it hadn't opened I was so relieved. I took his hand. "Thank you very much," I said my whole body now shaking.

"We were bloody lucky, but you shouldn't have been out here at all!" he still sounded angry. The relief of getting in the shelter was wonderful. I turned around to thank the warden once again still holding his hand, but it wasn't the warden, the man was a complete stranger!

While Mother gave out the scones I related all that had happened, my voice hoarse with shock, but Mother brushed me aside,

"Well you're alright now that's all that matters. Here you are, have a scone." I didn't feel hungry anymore and I still couldn't stop shaking. I went to find Jean as I knew she'd be interested.

A Dot's Life by Dorothy Buchanan

We had a week of fierce air raids after that. Bombs were falling in almost every area of Liverpool. It was called the "May Blitz" and the city centre was almost demolished. Houses, even streets were completely destroyed. Our school was bombed and badly damaged, so we couldn't go to school. Grandma Phillips' house was bombed during that week too, so badly, she couldn't live there again. Everyone knew someone who'd been "Bombed Out" as it was called.

Grandma Phillips came to stay with us and Granddad went to stay with Aunty Mary. I thought Grandma would be very upset, but she joked about not having to put up with Granddad for awhile. When the sirens went the following night, Grandma flatly refused to go in the shelter and Mother insisted I stay with her. We sat opposite each other in armchairs, not under the table as Dad instructed.

"Don't worry Dolly. If your name's on the bomb you'll get it," she joked.

I didn't feel as frightened as I thought I might, but I missed going to the shelter and seeing my friends. After an hour or so she said she was going upstairs to bed.

"No Jerry is going to deprive me of my bed." She made her way upstairs to my bedroom. I was sleeping on a bed chair in the living room while she stayed with us. When Mother and Dad returned from the shelter they were surprised to find both Grandma and I fast asleep!

Chapter Nine
Mailer, Scraps and Fruit

I was enjoying being off school and I thought I'd never have to go again. That pleasure didn't last long as we were informed classes could take place in some pupils' houses while the classrooms were being repaired. Many parents offered the use of their front parlours, but most were too small to house many children. June Furlong's house was chosen to take some of our class, as her house was larger than most. Even so, only ten pupils were taught at one sitting.

June's house was lavishly furnished and we all sat around a long highly polished table in awe of her lovely home. We spent most of the time admiring all the unusual ornaments and carvings her seafaring Uncle had brought home from foreign countries. We had different teachers daily, so the school work was haphazard and classes only lasted two hours. Reading or writing were the only two subjects taken and we quickly became bored with the lessons and our surroundings. Happily this arrangement was short lived as some of the classrooms were patched up - ours being one of them. Although there had been a lot of bomb damage to the school, we soon got accustomed to our makeshift classrooms with broken doors, chipped walls, boarded windows and a great deal of dust. It didn't bother us at all.

One family, who had lost their home in the bombing, were housed next door to the "Bad House." Jean made it her business to find out all about them.

"They have a boy called Billy," she came running to tell me. "His Mother and Father look really old but he's got a smashing' dog. You should see it, it's really friendly too." Jean loved being the first with information.

Soon afterwards we saw Billy and his dog in the street. I asked him the dogs' name. "Mailer," he said. It was a medium sized brown mongrel, with a lovely kind sort of face. Jean and I called him and he came bounding over, licking us all over, he certainly was friendly!

A Dot's Life by Dorothy Buchanan

Billy was slightly older than most of us and he had a vivid imagination telling us weird and wonderful stories about himself. At first we were amused and pretended to believe him, but we soon tired of the game. However, we all liked his dog, "Mailer," as he was very clever - and when we played rounders, we didn't need a fielder as he'd always fetch the ball for us!

Every day he was out roaming the streets, he seemed to feed on anything anyone gave him. We shared our sweets and any bits of food we had, with him. He soon attached himself to us and followed us everywhere; even when we went to the local shops we'd find him behind one of us.

A few times he followed me to school and bounded around with the children having a fine time in the play ground. The old caretaker wasn't pleased as it took him ages to catch him, and push him out of the school gate which was always locked after we were all in school.

One day Billy told us "Mailer" would have to be put down as his parents didn't want him anymore. We didn't know whether to believe him or not, but it turned out to be true. We were all very upset, but Billy wasn't a bit perturbed.

"I'm not bothered. We'll be getting an "Alsatian" soon, because my Mam likes them better than mongrels." We didn't believe him, neither were we interested what he was going to get. Mailer was our main concern. If only we could find him a good home as we hated to think he might be put down. He'd survived all the bad raids too (Billy told us he was outside in all of them - but we doubted that). I decided to try and persuade Mother and Dad to have him, but Mother always said *dogs cause too much mess*. During tea that evening I told them the sad story of Mailer, stressing what a friendly obedient dog he was (which was a slight exaggeration) but I'd have said anything to sway them. Then I chanced asking them outright.

"Why don't we have him? I'd look after him. He knows me and he'd be no trouble at all?" Mother said no, immediately, but Dad gave me a glimmer of hope.

"I often see that dog on my way home from work and it

does seem friendly enough." I went on and on about all the smart things Mailer could do. I was desperate to persuade them.

"You'll be safer with a dog in the house when Dad is on nights too" I said. Mother didn't answer, but Dad said-

"Yes that's true. We'll see anyway." That sounded far more hopeful. I carried on each day talking about Mailer. Grandma even backed me up a few times, which I was pleased about, but Mother gave her a frozen look and said "Cyril and I have to make decisions in this house Mother, nobody else!" Grandma looked at me and pulled a face without Mother seeing. Later on she whispered-

"I'm only a lodger here and I have to keep my nose clean, just like that dog - if ever it comes here!" She gave a knowing grin as she spoke. I really hoped they were considering having Mailer, as Dad had said. But time was running out.

A few days later while eating breakfast, Mother said casually,

"Dad and I have decided to have that dog, for a trial period only. Remember, if it's any trouble, it's off to the Dog's Home!" I was so thrilled I wanted to hug her. Instead I thanked her over and over again, until she told me to stop being so silly saying-

"All this fuss about a dog." I could hardly wait to get out of school that day.

Mailer was in the street as usual when I got home and I went to tell Billy's mother we would have him. She didn't seem at all interested and just said *fine*, and closed her door. I proudly took Mailer home, with a piece of string for a lead. Mother was at the front door-

"He looks as if he could do with a good bath," she said inspecting him carefully. "Here are some bits for him." She gave me some scraps of left-overs on a tin plate.

"It's your job to feed him every day. I'm far too busy, but I'll keep the leftovers for him - and don't forget to wash the plate afterwards." That didn't worry me. At last I had my own dog to care for! Dog food wouldn't be bought, but he was used to eating scraps.

Mailer seemed to sense he was on trial - he behaved very well. From early morning until late afternoon he was outdoors, as he was a street dog. I think this suited Mother perfectly. When he finally

A Dot's Life by Dorothy Buchanan

decided to come in, he'd eat his food and sleep under the table for the rest of the night. I was so relieved; he proved no trouble I was in my element. Everything was wonderful! I loved him very much. Billy and his family moved house soon afterwards and this really pleased me as I often worried in case they'd want him back.

Some days Mailer would wait by the school gate for me and everyone made a big fuss of him. I was very proud and took him everywhere I could. I felt happier than I'd ever been!

Grandma and Granddad Phillips were at last allocated rooms over an Insurance office in Smithdown Road. Everyone who had lost their homes were given some sort of alternative accommodation and Mother and Dad spent a lot of time with her, making it comfortable. She only had two rooms; a bed sitting room and kitchen no bathroom. A flight of wooden steps from the outside veranda led to her lavatory. In bad weather a bucket had to be used. It was always "bad weather" as far as Grandma was concerned! Granddad had moved back in with her and they carried on much as before, arguing and shouting. But they settled in their new small flat quite quickly. I believe Grandma enjoyed having her bed in the living room, she would often be lying in it when we visited. If Mother asked her why she was in bed, she'd say-
    "Oh, I had an awful headache Maud," and give me a wink!

I now had my own bed again it seemed much softer than I remembered, probably because the Bed Chair was so hard! Rationing was still in force and it was difficult to make the amounts of food allocated to each person stretch out the week. I hated only being allowed half a teaspoon of sugar in my tea, and Mother mixing the margarine and butter ration together, to make it last! She worked out all our rations with meticulous precision. Aunty Milly offered to let us have extra butter and sugar she got on the Black Market. It was double the price of course, but lots of people bought it. Mother was adamant-
    "I'm not having anything illegal, so tell her to keep it!"
Aunty Milly thought she was stupid. "I'm thinking about you growing children," she used to say.
"She can go without if she wants to, but she has no right to deprive

children!" she was annoyed. It was often offered but Mother always refused.

Fruit was in very short supply too, but each time we visited Grandma and Aunt Milly, we would be given two big bags of fruit; usually Pears, Apples and Plums. David and I were always pleased. No Bananas or Oranges of course, nobody got those, until the war finished. Greengrocers were sent a small quantity of fruit, but only occasionally. Aunty Milly always kept most of her allocation for us. Her customers must have been the losers, but Mother accepted the fruit without question.

Chapter Ten
A Letter for Dad and Chores for Me

A few months after my eleventh birthday, in 1941 a letter arrived for Dad with O.H.M.S on the envelope, it contained his calling up papers. He was shocked. He never thought he'd have to join the forces. Neither did anyone else. He and Mother couldn't believe it. They kept reading the letter over and over again.

"I didn't think they would ever call up men of your age; your nearly thirty eight!" she kept saying.

"Don't worry love, I doubt if I'll pass the medical," Dad looked hopeful, but the letter was fluttering in his trembling hands. Mother began to cry-

"How would I manage here on my own, if you're called up?" she wailed. Dad did his best to comfort her. Then I intervened-

"Lots of my friends' Dad's have gone in the Army and their Mother's manage alright." She stopped crying for a minute, then snapped, "That's because the majority of women around here are glad to see the back of them. I happen to have a good husband!" I didn't know what else to say.

I went out to tell my friends the sad news and much to my surprise, most of them were impressed. "I'll bet your Dad's proud, being called up" said one of them. I'd never thought that, but I began to think about it differently. Dad passed his medical, much to his surprise and was to join the Royal Army Service Corp. and report to a camp in Matlock, Derbyshire, within the week. After three months he would have seven days leave. Mother was inconsolable. She cried every day after receiving the news. Dad tried his best to reassure her, to no avail. I went with him to say his farewells to Grandma and Aunty Milly. I was pleased they didn't cry, although they looked sad.

"Look after yourself Cyril," they shouted from the doorstep. "Don't forget, if there's anything you need let us know, and write regularly." I didn't feel sad at all, I felt proud. My Dad like lots of my friends Dads was going to fight for our country!

A Dot's Life by Dorothy Buchanan

The day he left was dreadful. Mother became hysterical, clinging hold of him, sobbing-

"You can't leave me on my own like this!" Poor Dad hadn't any idea how to cope with her and looked as if he was going to cry himself. He kept repeating

"I have to go love. I have no choice. You've got the children, you'll be alright." I felt angry with Mother and thought she should have been proud of him, like I was.

The next few days after Dad left were awful. Mother did her usual household chores but didn't make any meals. We had sandwiches and pies for quite some time. She was always tearful, and writing daily letters to Dad. My role in the home altered considerably too. I hadn't realised how reliant she was on Dad.

One early evening I came in after playing to find her sitting in the dark.

"I've been calling you for ages. Where have you been?" she demanded.
Before I had time to reply, she said-

"I don't know what we're going to do. The light has gone out. I don't know how to fix a new bulb. Your Dad always did those jobs." I was surprised, as I'd seen Jean's Mother replacing a light bulb often. It didn't seem a difficult task. I was irritated.

"Give me the bulb and I'll put it in," I said, rather harshly. I climbed on a chair. It took me awhile to work it out in the dark and then I remembered Jean's Mother giving it a twist. At last the light came on, I was pleased with myself.

"That's a good girl. You'll have to help me as much as you can now your father's away," she said in a whining voice.

I inherited a lot of Dad's jobs; bringing a bucket of coal up from the cellar each day before going to school, cleaning all the sash windows standing on a chair. The bedroom windows were far more tricky - sitting outside on the window ledge, with the window pressed hard across my thighs and Mother instructing me from inside *not to forget the corners!*

A Dot's Life by Dorothy Buchanan

Dad was due home on leave and I was dying to see him in his uniform! I hoped we'd have a party as lots of my friend's mothers had big parties when their husbands came home on leave! Mother was horrified at the suggestion. I tried my best to persuade her-

"It would be a great welcome home for him."

"Your Father doesn't want that sort of welcome home. Seeing us will be enough for him."

Dad arrived home, unexpectedly.

"I didn't think you would be home until tomorrow," Mother greeted him. I was shocked at how different he looked. His hair had been cut high above his ears, his forage hat sat precariously on the side of his balding head. When he hugged me, his khaki uniform felt very coarse and smelt of straw. He had white gaiters, heavy black boots and lots of brass buttons and badges. Mother made him a cup of tea while he related all his exploits of the past three months. It looked odd seeing him in his usual chair dressed as he was. He looked like a stranger.

He spent the evening telling us how he'd been trained to kill with a bayonet and how gruelling the exercises were; the exhausting manoeuvres in a forest, for days on end. I listened fascinated, but Mother stopped him-

"It upsets me to hear all this. You're home now and you should forget all that." Dad looked hurt.

"Sorry love, but that's been my life for the past few months." He chose not to talk about his experiences again, much to my disappointment.

The week passed very quickly, I dreaded the day he'd go back to camp. Mother was again grief stricken and Dad was very quiet. I hated these scenes. Home life was miserable again. Dad's letters brought a bit of cheer, but it was short lived.

Chapter Eleven
Mailer and the Adoption Papers

Coming home from school one day, I was surprised not to see Mailer in the street as I usually did; I assumed he must be in the house.

"Mailer," I called as Mother opened the door.

"He's not here," she said.

"Well he isn't outside either," I was worried.

"I wonder where he could be? I'll go and look for him."

"You don't need to look for him. Get in." She pushed me along the hall.

"I took Mailer to Grandma's this afternoon. He's staying there for a while."

"PARDON!" I shrieked. I couldn't believe it! "You took Mailer to stay with Grandma?"

"Yes, and don't speak to me in that tone of voice. Grandma will be safer in that flat with a dog." Mother seemed very matter of fact about it.

"I'm going to bring him back home right now!" Tears were rolling down my cheeks as I made my way to the front door.

"You'll do no such thing." Mother was shouting now, pushing me back into the living room.

"He stays there for the time being and that's it. I don't want to hear another word about it!" I sobbed hysterically I couldn't believe Mother could do such a thing.

"You can't do this to me, he's my dog. I love him. You said I could have him; you *never* keep promises!" I was yelling at her now.

"You're the meanest Mother in the world. You *always* stop me having good things and do you know what, *I really HATE you!*" Mother clenched her teeth, I felt frightened of what she was going to do. She grabbed me by the shoulders, her nose almost touching mine,

"Don't you dare speak to me like that, do you hear? You get far more than most children around here and still you're not satisfied!" Her words splashed my face. "If your Father heard you,

A Dot's Life by Dorothy Buchanan

he'd give you a damn good hiding. Now get out of my sight before I lose my temper!" I sobbed and tried to explain how much Mailer meant to me but it made no difference. I knew she wasn't going to change her mind.

I didn't believe I'd ever have Mailer back again. I stayed in my bedroom most of the evening, feeling very upset and thinking all the time about poor Mailer. I wished Mother would understand how unhappy she'd made me. Crying myself to sleep I began to wonder if I was adopted? Especially with all the nasty things she'd done, like not letting me be a bridesmaid, being horrible to Jean, and now, worst of all, giving Mailer away although she knew I loved him so much.

I thought about these things over and over again. *Surely* I reasoned, *if you love someone you would want them to be happy?* I convinced myself Mother didn't care whether I was happy or not. I MUST be adopted. That seemed to make sense! I decided I'd find out as soon as I could, and then find my real Mother. There must be papers or something about it in the house?

Mailer found his way home from Grandma's, on two occasions that week. I was delighted to see him and he made such a fuss of me too. I was amazed how he'd found his way home. I was sure after the long journey he'd made to reach us, Mother would relent and allow him to stay. But in spite of my tears and pleadings, on each occasion Mother took him back to Grandma's almost immediately.

I went to see him often, but I always came away having a cry to myself. She liked him and treated him well, but I wished so much he was *my dog* again. Whatever Mother had said, I knew now he was going to be with Grandma forever. Although I loved visiting him I hated leaving him too and he'd look at me with doleful eyes, as if to say, "Why are you leaving me here?" It was heartbreaking.

Sometimes when Mother went shopping, she'd leave me at home on my own.
I welcomed these times; it gave me a chance to search for my adoption papers, which l felt sure must exist! I hunted through

drawers, boxes, and cupboards but found nothing, only old rent books and receipts. The only other place I'd seen her put things was on top of the wardrobe, in her bedroom. Standing on a bedroom chair, I reached up but there weren't any sort of papers there at all. I was disappointed, but there was a long leather bound box and, thinking it must contain a watch or necklace, I decided to have a look and opened it. Inside lay a rather big yellow rubber tube. One end looked like a baby's feeding bottle teat. I couldn't think what it was. I took it out and scrutinised it carefully. It was coated with what seemed to be talcum powder; my fingers got covered with it.

I was so absorbed I didn't hear Mother opening the front door. Then I heard her making her way upstairs to put her coat in the wardrobe (as she usually did). I was in a panic and didn't know what excuse to give, for being in her bedroom.

Without thinking clearly I quickly put the chair back in its place, but I still had the box and rubber tube in my hand when Mother entered the room, before she had chance to say anything, I blurted out-

"I was going to try on your shoes. But when I opened the wardrobe this box and thing fell off the top." Mother looked flustered and not annoyed as I'd expected. She seemed to believe my story too. I dangled the object in front of her-

"What's this for?" I asked. She looked embarrassed and went rather pink, then snatched it from me and put it quickly in the box and back on top of the wardrobe.

"Come on downstairs, and don't go in my wardrobe again!"

"But what's it for?" I persisted. She had her back to me walking down the stairs-

"Your Father uses it at work." I was puzzled, but decided not to ask any further questions.

Chapter Twelve
Burma and Parcels for Dad

Dad was due home on leave again, but this time it was Embarkation Leave - he was being sent overseas! Mother couldn't believe it. "God knows how long he'll be away this time - and overseas too."

I thought my friends would certainly be impressed with this news, I could hardly wait to tell them. Although Dad was also shocked at being sent overseas, he appeared excited by the prospect.

"There's a rumour we're being sent to the Far East. Some fellows think it might be Burma," he told us rather proudly.

"Burma! I thought it would be Germany. That's where most of the troops are." Mother looked surprised.

"No. If the rumour's right, we'll be fighting the Japs," Dad continued "That's why we've had all that hard training. The Japs are a different lot to the Germans. They're more ruthless." I listened in awe.

"Somebody said part of the journey would be by plane. I've never been out of England let alone going in a plane." I thought it sounded thrilling and wondered if I'd ever go anywhere in a plane? Dad seemed more worried about the plane journey than the destination.

The seven days leave passed quickly and Mother was worse than she'd ever been the day he left, she sobbed most of the morning. When the time came for Dad to say goodbye, tears were streaming down her face as she clung hold of him on the front step. I felt I should be crying too, but I didn't feel sad. I tried my best to force some tears, but no tears seem to be there. Then I thought of Mailer and a book I'd recently read, "Black Beauty" about a horse that had been badly treated and the tears soon flowed. My tears seemed to please Mother, she put her arm around me as we waved goodbye to Dad.

Mother continued to be rather helpless without Dad. If David fell or hurt himself in any way, she'd become very tearful and didn't

A Dot's Life by Dorothy Buchanan

seem able to cope. She'd call me in even if I was out playing, insisting I bathe or dress the cut or scratch.

"I'm too sensitive to do things like that," she'd say. I still did the other jobs in the house too, getting the coal from the cellar, replacing light bulbs, in fact most of the everyday chores Dad had always done.

Mother was depressed most of the time. All she seemed to talk about was Dad and most of her spare time was taken up writing letters to him, or waiting for the Postman. Dad's first letter took a long time to arrive. She read it out loud to David and I, then read it to herself quite a few times. The letter was heavily censored so there wasn't a lot of information, except about the intense heat, abundance of flies and the awful journey which took days, and how they were transported like cattle to their destination! But he seemed to have accepted the situation, and even joked about getting a suntan!

He had been sent to Burma as he thought, but we didn't know which part. The address had a lot of numbers and "Burma" at the end. When I visited Aunty Milly and Grandma Lawrence they were very pleased and relieved, as they'd also received a letter.

Aunty Milly told me she was trying to collect a few things to send him-

"Poor Cyril. Heaven knows what it must be like out there. He'll need a bit of cheering up," and she showed me the beginnings of a parcel she was preparing; writing paper, shaving soap, cigarettes and sweets (mostly things she'd bought on the Black Market)! She was making him a fruit cake too. I thought this was a really good idea, but when I told Mother she was livid! She said *if Dad needed anything it was HER place as his wife to send it, not Aunty Milly's!* I was tempted to tell her that she wouldn't be able to get all the things Aunty Milly could, but I thought it best not to say anything.

A few weeks later Aunty Milly told me she'd received a letter from Mother telling her *not to send Dad any more parcels*, stressing *it was her job to send Dad anything he needed, not hers!* Aunty Milly and Grandma were incensed. They both thought Mother had no right to dictate to

A Dot's Life by Dorothy Buchanan

them what they should send Dad.

"That's typical of your Mother. Whatever your Father saw in her I'll never know," Grandma said. I felt so ashamed. I wished Mother hadn't written such an awful letter!

Chapter Thirteen
Jean's Secret and Uncle Leslie's Illness

Quite a few classrooms at school had been patched up - the Science room being one of them. Elsie and I hated Science, perhaps because we were frightened of the Science master. He was extremely strict. If you weren't paying attention he'd throw a piece of chalk at you or the wooden chalk duster! If you were caught talking during the lesson, he'd send you to the Headmaster for the cane. I had the cane a few times for talking, but I never told Mother - she'd have said I must have deserved it!

Elsie and I became more aware of the boys in our class and they were certainly interested in us. We often got love notes passed down the section to us with messages like, "Kenny Wilson wants to kiss you" or something similar. We became very blasé and pretended we weren't interested, but we loved the attention and began to take a great interest in our appearance. We put Vaseline on our eyelids and lips to make them shine and curlers in our hair at night. We thought we looked lovely and spent lots of time consulting mirrors. I passed on our beauty tips to Jean but she only laughed-

"You wouldn't catch me putting muck on my face." She enjoyed being a tomboy.

One day while we were playing in the street she whispered-

"I've got something to tell you." I couldn't imagine what she was about to tell me then she cupped her hand over her mouth so nobody else would hear, and whispered "Don't tell anybody, but we're "Shifting!" I was surprised and saddened.

"Where are you shifting to?" I whispered back.

"I don't know. They won't tell me," she said looking mysterious. I wondered if this was a figment of her imagination. She enjoyed dramatising things.

She didn't mention it again so I didn't think any more about it. A few weeks later on my way to call on Jean I noticed a lot of neighbours outside her house huddled together in groups talking. I

A Dot's Life by Dorothy Buchanan

wondered what had caused the interest. Jean will know I thought, as I knocked on her door.

"It's no use you knocking there love," one of the women shouted. "The house is empty. They've done a "Moonlight Flit!" They were all talking quite loudly now.

"No wonder they scarpered, owing such a lot of rent; they owed money to everyone!" Another woman said nastily. I was shocked. My best friend had gone after all. Nasty remarks about Jean's family were thrown around and as I looked back at the windows I couldn't believe Jean was longer there.

"They never told a soul either," shouted someone. Well she told me, I thought, but I felt stunned as I walked slowly back to our house.

I didn't repeat the gossip I'd heard to Mother. I just told her Jean and her family had left.

"That was a quick move," she said suspiciously.

I didn't play in the street much after that. I missed Jean a lot. I didn't see any friends from the shelter either, as the raids had almost stopped in Liverpool. I began to spend more time with school friends. Nobody found out where Jean and her family had moved to. I never saw her again.

Each month Mother went to Bibby's (the factory where Dad had worked) to collect an allowance they granted to their employees in the forces. David and I usually went with her and on one of these outings Mother decided to have our photographs taken to send to Dad. It was obvious lots of people had the same idea. The queue outside "Jerome's" (the photographers in London Road) was long. It was a hot sticky day and the wait was awful. David felt sick and became very weepy. I lifted him up and tried to comfort him, unfortunately he vomited all over me! Mother wasn't pleased but she did her best to tidy us up with her spitted handkerchief. The foul smell of vomit lingered with me all day. We waited for the picture to be developed which again took ages. However the picture was reasonably good, or so Mother thought. Although, David looked fragile, almost angelic, with his pale white face and long platinum blonde curls. I had deliberately tried to adopt a pose, but now I could see how silly I looked. I didn't like the picture at all, I was glad nobody else would see it. Mother sent it off to Dad in her next letter.

Aunty Milly met David and I one Sunday as usual, but on this occasion she looked very upset. I could tell she'd been crying. I couldn't think why.

"I'm afraid I have some bad news to tell you," she said in a strained voice. "Your poor Uncle Leslie is very ill and the Air Force have sent him straight home to hospital." She looked as if she would burst into tears at any moment.

"What's the matter with him?" I asked. I couldn't imagine Uncle Leslie being ill, he was so young, handsome and fit looking. She looked very worried-

"They don't know yet, but let's hope he soon improves." We didn't spend long with her that day. She was anxious to visit him. Mother was surprised to see us back so soon. I told her the news right away, but she didn't seem very interested.

"You'll have to write and tell Dad about Uncle Leslie being ill," I said.
"I'll tell your Father in my own good time. I don't need you or anybody else to tell me what I should do," she replied.

We didn't see or hear from Aunty Milly for a few weeks and I couldn't understand why she hadn't been waiting for us as she usually did each Sunday on the corner?
Then Mother received a letter, informing her of Uncle Leslie's death and funeral arrangements. I was very shocked and sad to hear the news. I never thought Uncle Leslie would die.

"It will be ages before Dad finds out," I said. Mother was still reading the letter.

"Yes it will," she said, putting the letter on the sideboard. "Anyway, I won't be going to any funeral." I was shocked-

"Why aren't you going?" I thought with Dad being away, Mother would want to be there in his place.

"I have no intention of going to THAT house whatever the circumstances!"

"But Uncle Leslie is Dad's brother - and he's dead!" I shouted. I couldn't understand how she seemed to take the news so nonchalantly. She folded the letter back in its envelope and put it in the drawer and continued with her polishing, as if she hadn't heard me. There was a long silence. Then without turning around, she said-

"You can go to his funeral if you want to."

"Me? On my own?" I was startled and frightened. I'd never been to a funeral. I didn't know what to expect. All the stories Jean had told me flashed through my brain. She'd said everyone kept dead relatives in the parlour in an open coffin, so all family and friends could say their last goodbyes. She'd also said some of her relatives kissed the dead person and expected her to do the same! It sounded horrendous to me. I'd never really believed her, but now I was having doubts. Much as I'd liked Uncle Leslie, I didn't want to see him or kiss him, now he was dead!

Chapter Fourteen
Uncle Leslie's Farewell

I decided to attend Uncle Leslie's funeral, although I was still frightened, I didn't know what to expect. I thought Aunty Milly would be pleased to see me, with Mother refusing to go.

The journey to Grandma's house seemed much shorter than usual as my mind was full of awful thoughts. Mother had given me a bunch of flowers to take and I had clutched them so tightly they already looked wilted. I was shaking when I knocked on the door. The door was opened by Aunty Milly. She looked shocked to see me, but gave me a weak smile.

"Oh Dorothy it's you. I thought your Mother would have come. This is no place for a young girl!" She was dressed in black and looked awful. Her face looked puffy and her eyes were red and swollen. "Come on in dear, we'll go in the kitchen" I closed my eyes tightly as I rushed along the hall, I didn't want to see in the parlour! Aunty Milly ushered me into the kitchen where Grandma sat by the table looking extremely old and frail.

"You can stay with Grandma. We'll all be going soon" She tried her best to sound normal but her voice was faltering. "Are you sure you don't want to see Leslie, Mother?" Grandma became tearful and angry-

"How many more times are you going to ask me? I've told you. I want to remember him as he was!" I was relieved. If I were asked I'd know what to say.

Grandma and I sat in silence at the kitchen table. Muffled voices and shuffling noises could be heard in the hall. After a while we heard the front door close, which prompted Grandma to bury her face in her handkerchief and sob bitterly. I didn't know what to say or how to comfort her.

"You go in the other room now Dorothy, I'll be alright," she said, her hands still pressing the handkerchief over her face. I knew she wanted to be alone and I was pleased to leave her. I went into the living room, then, slowly ventured into the empty parlour.

A Dot's Life by Dorothy Buchanan

The floor was amassed with petals. the sweet fragrance of flowers was overwhelming. I pulled open the curtains, the sun was shining and my fears had now left me. I gathered some of the rose petals and put them in a glass bowl. I thought about Uncle Leslie, and how he used to make me laugh and how unhappy Aunty Daisy would be without him.

How terrible it must be for Grandma and Aunty Milly - and Dad doesn't even know! It was all very sad and so unreal. The strongest fragrance in the room was coming from a glass vase of tall white flowers on a table by the window. They were so perfect in colour and shape almost waxen, I thought they were artificial. I'd never seen them before.

Grandma called me from the kitchen and said she'd made some tea, I felt uncomfortable as she still looked as if she were about to cry again. To break the silence I told her how much I liked the lovely white flowers in the glass vase, this seemed to please her.

"Aunty Daisy bought those Lilies. They were very expensive too, but she wanted the best for Uncle Leslie. Bring them in here will you dear?" She said. I carried the vase carefully into the kitchen. She took her time stroking and admiring them.

"They are beautiful aren't they? Aunty Daisy brought them here the day dear Uncle Leslie came home for the last time." Tears began to roll down her cheeks again. She took one of them from the water.

"I want you to take this home," she said, between sobs.

"Press it in a heavy book and when you look at it you can remember Uncle Leslie." I thanked her and told her I would always treasure it, she wrapped it tenderly in tissue paper. She put her arms around me and hugged me for awhile.

"Dorothy, you've been a great comfort to me." I didn't know how. But I was pleased.

When everyone arrived back to the house Aunty Milly gave them all a drink of wine and Aunty Daisy served plates of sandwiches. She looked wretched, trying her best not to cry. I felt very sorry for them all and wished Mother had been there for them.
I noticed Aunty Milly hadn't eaten a thing and was unusually quiet.

A Dot's Life by Dorothy Buchanan

Then she surprised me-

"I think I should take you home now." After tearful goodbyes from Grandma and Aunty Daisy thanking me for coming, Aunty Milly suggested we get the tram to the Pier Head. I was surprised and pleased. I didn't want to go straight home. We caught a tram and then while we were sitting on the top deck front seats, Aunty Milly produced a Mars bar from her handbag.

"Here is a little treat for you. I could only get one and I think you deserve it" The thick sweet chocolate bar tasted wonderful. I thanked her over and over again. She was always so kind and thoughtful.

"This break away from the house is just what I needed," she said, taking in deep breaths of sea air as we walked along the Pier Head.

"I'm so glad you came, Dorothy. You've helped Grandma and me a lot today." I was pleased to hear her words but I couldn't understand how I had helped anyone? Nevertheless, I felt happy to be with Aunty Milly, in spite of the sadness of the day.

Mother asked me a lot of questions about the funeral when I arrived home, but I was very evasive. I felt angry and hurt she didn't attend the funeral. I thought she was very unkind.

Although I felt so sad that Uncle Leslie had died, I was pleased I'd gone to the house to see Grandma and Aunty Milly - and I didn't have to view Uncle Leslie after all. I don't know what illness he'd died of. When I asked Aunty Milly she'd said it was a tropical disease? But he'd never been abroad? Years later, I found out he'd died of cancer of the stomach.

Chapter Fifteen
Miss Schneider and the Job Hunt

A lot of changes had taken place at school. We were going into our last year now, being thirteen. In those days, everyone left school at fourteen. We lost touch with the children who had gone to colleges when they were eleven, June furlong being one of them.

College fees were high and not many parents could afford them. The rest of us never felt in the least bit envious. In fact, we felt rather sorry for them, having to make new friends. Our final year teacher was Miss Schneider; a slim, dark-haired elegant lady in her forties, very refined and cultured, never aggressive, but persuasive and quietly spoken. She was highly respected and never seemed to shout or lose control. We were all pleased to be going into her class. Some children said she was German, but that didn't matter to us, although none of us liked Germans after the bombing. She had an air of grandeur about her Had we been told she was really "Lady Somebody" we would have believed them, without question.

We didn't do any of the usual school work on our first day. Instead, she spent the time telling us how to make the most of our abilities and how she would spend time with each of us, finding our potentials. She emphasised the importance of manners, literature and reading. None of us had any experience of this kind of teaching. The class was captivated.
"I like to feel proud of my class. I don't tolerate rudeness from anyone, I am here to help you with anything and everything you want to know." She then ended the lesson.

During the next few weeks she taught us more than we'd ever thought possible. Most of the subjects, which we'd found boring in previous classes, now took on a new dimension. She had a keen sense of humour which made learning easy and fun.
We were introduced to authors, playwrights, poets, painters. She discussed our interests, ambitions and explained how we should conduct ourselves in different circumstances. Nothing seemed

beyond her capabilities! We developed more confidence. She listened intently to our opinions and discussed them in depth. School was now a pleasure! Elsie, a friend of mine, and I, talked about Miss Schneider at length. We didn't, of course, know anything of her private life, but we invented stories that seemed fitting, mostly tragic romantic ones!

Some Saturdays I went to Elsie's house for the afternoon and we'd spend our time trying out new hairstyles or cutting out film star pictures from the "Picturegoer" magazine. Another pastime was reading the problem pages of Women's magazines and scanning them for *free offers* samples. It was always a thrill to have a package addressed to you containing soaps, toothpastes, deodorants *and even sanitary pads*, which neither of us required, but we kept them hidden until our great day arrived!

Lots of girls at school boasted about starting their periods although nobody used the word *periods*. Most used silly names like "The Curse" "Country Cousins" or "Poorly" which, after a while, Elsie and I copied. But we were still waiting patiently for ours!

When my "time" finally arrived I felt very grown up and proudly told Mother. She surprised me by not making any comments at all. She just opened the sideboard cupboard and produced a bundle of pads made from strips of sheeting crudely stitched together - all different shapes and sizes and two safety pins!

"You can use these," she said placing then on the table. I was disgusted.

"I'm not using things like that! I've got those samples I sent for." But Mother was adamant-

"I have no intention of wasting my money buying you those things. These can be washed and used over and over again. You just put them in salt water overnight, then wash them the next day." I remembered seeing them drying on the clothes line in the yard but I'd always thought they were dusters!

"I don't care, I'm not using them. I'll buy my own!" I shouted. Although I didn't know how I would be able to buy them. I'd go messages or clean some more steps, I thought. I was determined to get the money somehow rather than use those

A Dot's Life by Dorothy Buchanan

dreadful things Mother had made.

"If they're good enough for me, they are good enough for you," she snapped. I never used them, much to her annoyance.

I badly wanted to have a party for my fourteenth birthday. I had it all planned. I'd invite five boys and four girls from my class. I'd already been to a few of their parties and we'd had a great time. Mother wasn't keen on the idea and I kept reminding her that I'd never EVER had a birthday party! I nagged and moaned daily; she must have been fed up listening to me. Eventually she agreed, and I was more than delighted!

With rationing and food still in short supply, a birthday cake was out of the question. But Mother said she would make sandwiches and bake scones. Some of the parties I'd attended had carrot cake, which I thought tasted lovely, but Mother wasn't very inventive or interested in cooking. That didn't worry me, I was more interested in what we would do after the tea! I asked my friends in class for ideas and they suggested *Postman's Knock*, *Truth or Dare* and *Consequences*, but the most interesting idea was Marjorie's, "I'll dress up as a Fortune Teller, and tell their fortunes." We all agreed this a great idea and quite unique. We talked about how we'd organize it for ages.

Marjorie, from our class was very attractive, with olive skin and thick black flowing hair. Her Father was Portuguese. We all agreed she'd be just right for the role of *"Gypsy Zelda"*, the fortune teller we'd invented! She loved acting too and was always dramatic about every day events. She said she could get a long colourful dress. We would collect as much jewellery as we could and even managed a coin necklace that she could wear across her forehead over a scarf like a Bandanna. She'd look convincing. One of the girls had a wind up gramophone and records which she said she'd bring, so the party couldn't fail! It was a few months off yet, but I was pleased we had it all arranged.

As we were due to leave school at Christmas, which wasn't far off, Miss Schneider concentrated her attention on our future careers. Everyone had lots of private talks with her. I told her I wanted to

A Dot's Life by Dorothy Buchanan

be a hairdresser, and that the hairdresser my Mother attended each week had offered me a job there. She was horrified. I was surprised at her reaction.

"Don't even consider it!" She said with conviction. I was puzzled, I thought she'd have been pleased to hear I'd found myself a job, then she went on,
"Dorothy, local hairdressers could never give you the training a top salon could. On Saturday I want you to go to all the hairdressers in Bold Street and ask them if they require an apprentice. I will give you a character reference to take with you." Bold Street was considered a very high class shopping area. I never thought I would be able to work there.

The following Saturday I decided to take her advice. Mother thought it a ridiculous idea and a waste of time; especially, as I'd been offered a job already.

"Those places want a lump sum of money to teach you, and we can't afford that. My hairdresser would teach you for nothing, *and* give you a small wage!" she shouted. She wasn't pleased with Miss Schneider's suggestion. I understood what she meant. But Miss Schneider had given me a new goal.

I took my time getting ready for the big event, trying my best to look more grown up. I put my hair up in sweeps (as it was called) rubbed my cheeks to make them glow, put the usual vaseline on my lips and eyelids. I really thought I looked lovely. There must have been six or seven hairdressing Salons in Bold Street and I decided to call on them all!

I hovered outside the first shop for quite some time, dreading going in, but then I remembered Miss Schneider's words. The inside looked very grand. A lady with lovely hair and long red nails sat at a desk.

"Can I help you?" she drawled.

"I would like to know if you need an apprentice at the moment?" I said trying to sound very refined I could feel my cheeks burning.

"We do take apprentices, but there is a fee required for training. Can I take your name and address?" I panicked. I was

A Dot's Life by Dorothy Buchanan

frightened of giving my name and address in case it committed Mother to something. I muttered something like *it doesn't matter*, and hastily went out with my heart thumping. This was more difficult than I thought.

Most of the salons made the same comments, but I wasn't deterred. I was gradually gaining confidence and began to enjoy seeing inside these lovely salons. I now realised I would love to work in one of these shops they were so different from the one Mother frequented each week. Then I noticed another hairdressing Salon, on the first floor of the Lloyds Bank building on the corner of Seel Street (a side street off Bold Street). "Vincents" it said, in big gold letters across a cast iron balcony. I ran up the stone steps to the first floor and arrived at a big glass door with the same gold lettering as the front. A lovely aroma of perfume seemed to welcome me and I was very impressed with the large display cabinet and glass counter containing hair pieces, jewelled hair slides, sparkling tiaras and unusual shaped perfume bottles. It was very overwhelming. I decided to ask to see the manager this time. Something I hadn't done before.

"Do take a seat," said the lady at the counter. She was smiling warmly. I sat down and thumbed through a magazine I'd never seen before, "The Tatler" it was called. It was full of pictures of ladies in evening dresses attending parties. A small middle aged gentleman with a white, high necked silk overall approached me.

"I understand you want to see me. I am Mr. Vincent," he said. I stood up and we shook hands.

"Good afternoon Mr. Vincent. I am Dorothy Lawrence," I thought Miss Schneider would be proud of me. "I would like to be an apprentice here," I said, as quickly as I could.

"That's very interesting, but are you aware, high fees have to be paid for the privilege?" I was getting used to this reply, but his accent surprised me, it sounded Italian or Spanish?

"Well, I can't pay any fees but I'd still like to learn hairdressing here." He surprised me by laughing heartily, then, stood back looking at me for a moment. I wondered why he thought it funny.

"Come into my office and we'll have a little chat." I followed him to a tiny office at the back of the salon. "Sit down,

A Dot's Life by Dorothy Buchanan

and tell me why you think I should take you on as an apprentice?" I hadn't expected a question like this, but I was pleased.

"I've always wanted to be a hairdresser and my teacher told me only to apply to the best shops. That's why I'm here!" I pushed my reference across to him. He quickly read it, and looked up smiling. I didn't know what to think. There was a long pause, then to my amazement he said

"I admire your cheek. It's not often I meet a young girl with such spirit. Against my better judgement, I'm going to take you on. How do you feel about that?" He studied me intently.

"Oh, thank you very much," I said. "That's marvellous!" I kept wondering if I'd heard correctly?

"I will pay you seven and sixpence a week for the first year and, if you do well, there will be an increase accordingly" He stood up and opened the office door, then called someone named "Gertrude." Almost immediately, a rather severe looking plump lady came into the office.

"This is my wife. She will tell you everything you need to know." He left us alone. Her stern look gave me the impression she didn't approve of the arrangement.

"When can you start, that's the first question?" She read my reference as she asked me.

"I don't leave school until Christmas. I'm not fourteen until January." I did my best to sound polite and pleasing.

"In that case, you can begin the first of January. You will need two white overalls and a packed lunch each day. The hours are eight forty five until six and half day on Saturday - and by the way, we don't tolerate lateness! I will send you a letter of confirmation shortly." She seemed in a hurry to end the interview but she was now smiling. She shook my hand and I thanked her very much. As I made my way out, I took another quick look at the luxury of the surroundings. I could hardly believe I was actually going to work in such a lovely place!

I dashed home to tell Mother. She was very surprised and impressed when I told her about Mr Vincent and how he'd said I didn't have to pay any money, and I'd be getting seven and sixpence a week!

"Wait until I tell Dad you're going to work in Bold Street.

A Dot's Life by Dorothy Buchanan

He'll be pleased with that news. You did well for yourself!" I was thrilled to hear Mother praise me and felt quite proud of myself too.

Nearly all the class had obtained jobs for themselves, Elsie as a colourist in a photographers; Marjorie as a clerk in an Insurance company and most of the boys were going to be apprentices in different trades. Everyone seemed happy about their future but sad to be leaving Miss Schneider. She complimented us all.

We all assembled in the main hall the day we left. The Headmaster, Mr Brown, gave a long talk about being on our best behaviour at all times, and not to forget the excellent teaching we'd all received, at St Margaret's.

Our class then looked across to Miss Schneider and most of us had tears in our eyes, Marjorie was actually sobbing. Then we sang a few familiar school songs, when we came to "Forty Years On" we realised for the first time, what the words meant, and most of us were crying. Back in our classroom Miss Schneider thanked us for being an excellent class, and gave us each a reference, which everyone received on leaving, as no exams were taken.

Marjorie, Elsie and I wanted to buy her a special gift, but sadly we didn't have much money. Finally we bought her a cheap little Jewel box. None of us liked it much, but it was all we could afford. We presented it to her just before leaving the classroom, she looked surprised. Tears came to her eyes as she opened it, handling it with great care she said "Thank you all, very much indeed. It's lovely." We all cried, then, took a last look at the classroom where we'd spent so many happy days. Each of us went home with heavy hearts.

It seemed strange not to be going to school again, but now I had my party to look forward to. I was having it much earlier than my actual birthday. Marjorie, Elsie and I planned it over and over again. We wanted everything to be perfect. Marjorie decided she'd tell everyone she couldn't stay long, then when everyone thought she had gone home, she'd dress herself up in our cellar. I would get everything ready, by switching off the light and lighting a candle. To begin the evening we'd play games, then, we'd dance to a few records. I think Marjorie was more excited than us, as she loved the drama of it all. When she did a dress rehearsal, we were amazed how realistic she looked. I didn't tell Mother all our plans. I just told her Marjorie was going to get dressed up in the cellar as a Fortune Teller and not to tell the others.

Everything was going to be perfect. I could hardly wait for my first birthday party.

Chapter Sixteen
Fortune Telling and Hairdressing

At last, the day of my party arrived. I was beside myself with excitement. Mother had made scones and managed to get some biscuits. The table was laden with these and neatly arranged fish paste sandwiches and jam butties - all on large plates with floral doyleys. I was pleased. She'd gone to a lot of trouble. I just wished I could have had a special dress for the occasion, but that wasn't possible.

My friends all arrived, giving me gifts; mostly packs of cards, puzzles, dominos and pencils as there weren't many things they could buy at the time. But I did get more birthday cards than ever before! I asked Mother if she would be getting me a present. She became angry and told me *not to be so greedy, the party was her present!*

During tea Mother asked them all questions, which I knew she would, but we did manage to talk amongst ourselves. Once tea was over I ushered them into the parlour to begin our games. *Truth or Dare* being the first. The boys were shy, but once they found the dare was to kiss someone, they were much more interested!
We all overcame any shyness, and enjoyed it all. Laughing at each others' attempts and making cat calls. Everything was in full swing, although we were making a lot of noise. Then the door opened and Mother came in. I thought she was going to ask us to be a bit quieter. The game stopped immediately, then, much to my dismay, she sat down. "Carry on with your game, don't let me stop you," she said. Everyone looked awkward, the room went quiet. Nobody knew what to do or say. I was really annoyed. How could we play our games with Mother watching?

"Look Mother we don't want you in here. Go back in the other room please!" I sounded far nastier than I intended. She immediately got up and went out, without a word. Everyone gave a sigh.
"I thought your Mother wanted to play *Truth or dare*," joked one of the boys, and peals of laughter broke out. Our game

A Dot's Life by Dorothy Buchanan

continued, and then we played records and did a bit of dancing, then enjoyed all the other games we'd planned. We were all having a great time. It was almost time for Marjorie to pretend to go home. Marjorie gave me a wink, we made our goodbyes sound genuine, saying how sorry we were that she had to leave so early.

"You'll miss having your fortune told," shouted one of the boys. They seemed intrigued at the idea of a fortune teller coming, although most of them said they didn't believe in such rubbish. But they wanted to see her, just the same! I put the light out and lit the candle on the card table, hoping Marjorie wouldn't take too long getting ready. I left the room to check. When I went into the living room I was alarmed to find Mother hunched up in an armchair quietly sobbing pitifully into her apron.

"What's the matter?" I was worried. I thought something dreadful must have happened to Dad! She looked up her tear stained face all crumpled.

"It's you. You've upset me. Telling me you don't want me, after all I've done for you today!" I was relieved and exasperated.

"It's not that I don't want *you*, it's just that we're playing games, and you'd embarrass everyone being there" That seemed to make things worse.

"So you think I'd embarrass your friend's do you?" she began crying again. I didn't know how to explain what I meant and didn't try again. I just hoped that nobody had heard her crying. I felt embarrassed. I knew Marjorie must have heard everything, but she wouldn't say anything.

At that moment Marjorie came out of the cellar, she looked sensational. Her make-up, dress and jewellery were really convincing. She actually looked like a Fortune Teller. I was delighted at the transformation!

"Doesn't she look wonderful Mum," I tried to make my peace. Mother turned her head away and didn't reply. I tried very hard to put the episode out of my mind, but it bothered me for the rest of the evening.

"Here is Madam Zelda," I announced. Nobody guessed it was Marjorie. I could tell from their faces. She adopted a convincing foreign accent and delivered messages to them in hushed tones. She really was a good actress. Elsie and I had a job

A Dot's Life by Dorothy Buchanan

stifling our giggles. We were amused by the boys' faces as they all looked so impressed by her revelations. I had my turn last and sat opposite Marjorie, grinning. It had worked just as we'd planned. I knew Marjorie was enjoying herself, although the dim light hid her expression. I couldn't believe how attentive they'd all been.
Then, without warning the light went on, the full glare made Marjorie's disguise obvious! Mother stood in the doorway.

"It's about time you all went home," she shouted. But nobody was listening. The boys were pointing at Marjorie "We'll get you for this!" they teased.
Shrieks of laughter broke out as Mother left the room and banged the door. Everyone was talking at once.

I went with Marjorie to change. As we walked through the living room, Mother looked angry and yelled-

"Will you tell your friends to get off home. The noise is dreadful!"
Marjorie was irritated.

"It's a pity your Mother spoilt it all." I knew how she felt, I was disappointed too, but there was nothing I could do or say.

When they'd all gone home, Mother kept going on and on about how ungrateful I was, and how noisy they'd been. I tried my best to ignore her remarks and didn't answer her back. In spite of everything, I'd had my first birthday party that would be memorable.

The war was still on in Germany and Japan. Lots of service men had been killed. Most people knew someone who had lost their life. The raids had now stopped. Rationing was still in full force, but we were accustomed to it by now.

Christmas was a quiet affair. Children's toys and any type of gifts were in short supply. I felt sorry for David. Word got around that a shop in the city centre were selling toy cars. I queued for over an hour one morning and managed to buy a little blue car for him made of rubber. David was so pleased when he saw it on Christmas morning! It was well worth the wait!

A Dot's Life by Dorothy Buchanan

I was due to begin work on New Years' Day. Mother had managed to buy me the two white overalls that were required, but I was bitterly disappointed with her choice. They reminded me of those worn by fishmongers or butchers! They were long and made of thick white twill material with a cross-over front that tied at the back, and long sleeves which I would have to roll up. I'd also hoped to get a grown up outfit to start my job, but Mother insisted my navy blue school skirt and white blouse were suitable. To complete the outfit Mother produced a pair of shoes from her wardrobe, which she'd never worn. They were brown leather lace-ups with cuban heels in a very old fashioned style. I was upset about those but I had to wear them, as my school shoes had worn out. I just hoped that nobody would notice them.

I was up very early for my first day at work. I was excited as well as frightened. I hadn't any idea what it was going to be like. I ate my tea and toast quickly that morning and packed my overalls, lunch and school reference in a small shopping bag. Mother suggested I walk to work and get the tram home. I would have liked to have gone by tram, there and back, but she'd only given me enough money for one journey. However, although I still wasn't fourteen until the following week, I felt grown up and proud as I walked into town, with so many other people, going to work.

When I opened the door to Vincent's, the fragrance of perfumes and lotions met me again, but the confidence I had on that first visit, had now evaporated, I was trembling. I expected to see Mr. Vincent, but a middle aged lady met me, and introduced herself as Miss Barton. She seemed friendly and led me to the cloakroom.
"Put on your overall, and then come to the staff room," she said. I quickly changed. I was all fingers and thumbs and perspiring. The full length mirror wasn't encouraging either. I had imagined I looked far better! The overall was far too big and the sleeves seemed endless. It took me some time to roll them up. I began to feel worried about the time I was taking. One sleeve still hung lower than the other. Finally I made my way into the staff room.

A sea of faces met me, all sitting drinking tea around a large table,

A Dot's Life by Dorothy Buchanan

there must have been eight or nine, one girl being a similar age to me. They all looked very smart and attractive. I felt flustered, I'd gone quite red. Looking quickly around I realised I was the only person wearing such an old fashioned overall. Most wore thin cotton ones with delicate frills and gleaming silver buttons, some edged with frills of pink or blue. I felt ugly and out of place. They each said,

"How do you do?" While I said-

"Pleased to meet you," over again.

I was given a cup of tea, and a permanent place at the table. They resumed their conversations while I sat and sipped my tea. They all spoke in a refined way using words and phrases I'd not heard before. They were all what Jean and I used to call *posh people!*

I was told Mr and Mrs Vincent weren't in the salon that day, but Miss Barton was in charge. She gave me a list of the jobs I was expected to attend to each morning; check each of the twelve cubicles, make sure they were all tidy, with adequate supplies of shampoo, and setting lotions. One of the cubicles was not used for hairdressing it was more ornate than the others with what appeared to be green marble walls and lots of chrome. It had a long sofa in the centre draped with a white starched sheet. Different shaped gold topped bottles and jars adorned the sparkling glass shelves. A manicure tray on a small table contained every coloured nail polish. I loved all the selection of lipsticks, make up and eye shadows. I would certainly enjoy tidying here!

"This is Mrs Vincent's room, where she does her facials and manicures. So make sure it *always* looks clean and sparkling," Miss Barton explained. She also gave me a tour of the stock rooms, and told me I would be sharing other jobs, like making tea, washing dishes and running errands, with the other junior, "Annette." Then I would help one of the seniors with their clients. She suggested I help her, for the rest of the morning and stressed that whatever conversation took place between the hairdresser and the client must never be repeated to anyone. Neither were juniors expected to have any conversations with clients.

"All you have to remember is to be polite and always

address the client as Madam!" I listened intently. I ushered her clients into cubicles, took their coats, remembering to address them as Madam. Then I helped her, by passing pins or curlers and keeping everywhere tidy.

I had never seen so many well dressed ladies before. They all wore lovely outfits and some had heavy fur coats; most had lots of gold and diamond jewellery, and lovely wafts of perfume filled the air. One client had her chauffeur waiting in the lounge! I was really overwhelmed by everything.

The morning went by quickly, but I felt tired and hungry. Miss Barton said we could now have lunch-
"You've worked well Dorothy. I'm pleased with you." Her praise sounded wonderful! I collected my sandwiches from the cloakroom, and went to the staff room to take my allocated seat. We were the last to sit down for lunch, most had begun eating. I'd never seen such a varied selection of food before, chicken legs, boxes of salads, cold meats, cheeses, bread rolls wrapped in napkins, pots of honey, scones! I didn't know you could get such food?

My crumpled brown paper bag sat by my plate, I was loathed to open it. I took a gulp of tea, while I tried to work out how I should eat my sandwiches. Do I put them all on my plate, or take them out one at a time? I chose to put them all on my plate, what a mountain they made, they almost toppled over. The pungent smell of fish paste was overpowering. I hoped nobody else would notice. I felt as if everyone was looking at my castle of sandwiches. I kept my eyes on the plate, my face going redder each second. One of the seniors, Miss Beveridge asked if I'd like a piece of her chicken. I politely refused. I would have loved it of course, but I was too embarrassed to accept it. I ploughed through the sandwiches, I wasn't enjoying them but I was hungry.

The conversation flowed between the staff. They talked to me occasionally, but thankfully their attention was mostly with each other. Mother had put another small parcel at the bottom of the bag and I hoped it would be a scone or cake, but it was two jam butties.

A Dot's Life by Dorothy Buchanan

I was so relieved when the meal finished. I decided I'd ask Mother if she could give me some other kind of food for my dinner in future.

The following day, I helped Mr Vincent with his clients. I was very nervous when he asked me to *erase* a clients' appointment. I was in a panic I'd never heard the word *erase* before, I didn't know what it meant or what I should do. I came out of his cubicle and made my way to the appointment desk, the other junior Annette was there answering the phone. "Oh Annette" I whispered, "I have to erase an appointment for Mr Vincent." Before I could say anything else, she passed me the rubber and the appointment book. I could have hugged her! I soon learnt I could find a lot of things out this way.

The week went well. I loved it all, except lunch times; I hated opening those brown bags, with the inevitable meat of fish paste sandwiches, they were such an embarrassment.

I had asked Mother if she could give me something else in my sandwiches. She wasn't pleased and said,
"When you're earning decent money you can have what you like, and not until," adding that Dad had never complained whatever she'd given him. So I had to put up with them.

A small brown envelope with my name on was given to me on Saturday morning - my first weeks wage packet. Miss Barton said,
"You'll be rich this week Dorothy; most Mothers let you keep your first weeks wages!" I was surprised and excited I'd never heard that before! I dashed home from work feeling elated. I proudly gave Mother my unopened wage packet and watched her open it, then she took out two shillings.
"There's your tram fare, for the week." I was bitterly disappointed.
"I thought I'd be able to keep my wages for this week," I said.
"Well you thought wrong didn't you." I didn't tell her what Miss Barton had said.

Chapter Seventeen
Eric, the Witch and the Walk home

The following week, Mr Vincent decided my hair badly needed styling. I never thought I would be able to have my hair done there. I sat in the same chair as the rich clients I'd admired, with the same thick fluffy pink towels and lovely smelling lotions. Such a far cry from the weekly wash with Derbac soap over the kitchen sink!

My hair was carefully cut and set in a new style called a "Liberty Cut" like a curly bob. I could hardly believe it.
"What a transformation. She looks lovely." Miss Barton commented. I was surprised with all the attention I was receiving and enjoyed it. I proudly walked home that night, hoping everyone would notice my hair. I stopped at every shop window admiring my reflection. Mother was impressed with my new look too!
Each week I was able to have my hair done, I loved working at Vincent's, I was so pleased I had made the right decision.

Elsie and I were anxious to find something to do with our evenings. We didn't have much money so the choice was limited. We decided to join a Youth club at a church near Elsie's house. We felt a bit apprehensive going along to the church, but we were pleasantly surprised. A lady by the unusual name of Minnie Steinberg was the club leader. She introduced us to all the young fellows and girls; Joan, Flo, Lou, and Olive who quickly became our friends. As did the boys; Jimmy, Alfie, Billy and Eric. There was a varied selection of things to do; Badminton, Table Tennis, First Aid, Keep Fit and Drama classes, and the opportunity of going on holiday in the summer! The only drawback being, that we had to attend Church each Sunday. But Monday and Friday quickly became the highlights of our week!

We joined most of the classes we loved everything, especially the attention of the boys! After club we would stand talking, laughing and joking outside the church each of us girls enjoyed flirting with the boys; Jimmy, dark haired, cuddly and baby faced - he was a real

A Dot's Life by Dorothy Buchanan

charmer. Frank, the film star, we all thought he was handsome - so did he! Billy, the roughest of all, with a heart of gold - he'd help anyone. Then Eric, the boffin of us all, always quoting sayings or poetry none of us had heard of, but pretended we had!

Sunday evenings after church we'd usually go to Eric's house. His Mother was very easy-going and allowed us to dance in the living room. We'd roll up the mats, push the furniture against the wall and dance to a variety of records played on the gramophone. We'd dance with the boys and with Eric's Uncle who lived with them. He enjoyed showing us lots of fancy dance-steps. He said he was a professional dancer. Then before we went home, Eric's Mother would give us all a cup of cocoa.

The boys would walk each of us home, they were all very considerate - usually a different boy each time! When we reached home we would stand and talk for awhile then have a kiss and cuddle. Some of them seemed experienced with their kisses and become hot and bothered, it was very exciting!

One evening Eric and I were standing by the entry of Egerton Street kissing goodnight, we didn't hear my Mother coming; she frightened the life out of us by suddenly appearing. She was angry too.

"What time do you call this to be coming home?" I was shocked she looked like a witch with a black coat draped over her trailing nightdress her hair a mass of metal curlers but worst of all, she'd removed her false teeth!

"Get in immediately!" She spluttered, pushing me along the street. I was mortified!

"Sorry," muttered Eric to Mother "We didn't realise the time. Goodnight, see you at the club, Dot." He rushed quickly down the street. Mother began shouting after him.

"It's turned eleven o'clock. No decent young people stand in an entry this time of the night. Dorothy won't be seeing you in any club!" She glared at me. "I'm ashamed of you! What on earth do you think you're doing?"

"We were just talking and didn't realise how late it was, sorry." I tried to sound apologetic "Eric walked me home. He's one of the boy's from the club." As soon as we got indoors, Mother began ranting and raving-

"I don't believe you go to any church club. Those low down people you mix with wouldn't be allowed in any church! You'll stay in from now on!" I was infuriated.

"You've no rights to say nasty things about my friends. You don't even know them! I am still going to the club whatever you say, so you can just shut up!"
She looked as if she was going to hit me, but instead she threw herself on her knees and clasped her hands together in a praying position looking up to the ceiling.

"Please, *please* God, help me. What have I done to deserve an impudent daughter like this?" She said in a dramatic, moaning voice. I was shocked. I'd never seen her behave like this before. She wailed on, repeating her request to God. I didn't know what to do and quickly ran upstairs to bed before anything else happened. I couldn't understand why she'd gone to such extremes, just for being a bit late getting home. She wasn't interested in hearing any apologies either. The following morning I expected a lot of recriminations. I was very surprised that Mother never mentioned anything at all about the previous night. I was more than relieved though.

I went to the club as usual after that, but I was careful not to stay out late. I tried to interest her in all the things we did at the club, even inviting her to come one evening, which lots of Mother's had done, but she was disinterested.

Minnie, our club leader, told us she would like us to perform a play. There was a competition between the churches taking place in Central Hall, Renshaw Street, in the city centre. Most of the girls were interested, none of us had ever been in a play before and we wanted to try and win. Minnie had chosen a play called *"World Without Men."* I was given the part of an eccentric lady who loved *all* men. We each read our parts over and over again. We were determined it would be a success. We were lucky to have a professional lady dramatist to rehearse us, too.

We all loved acting it was a new experience for us. After six weeks

A Dot's Life by Dorothy Buchanan

intensive rehearsals we were ready for the dress rehearsal. I had to wear a shiny clinging long red dress and high heeled red shoes with a long white fur around my neck, all provided by our dramatist. It was very thrilling. I loved acting, and worked hard at perfecting the role. We were all given two complementary tickets for our family to see the show. This was my opportunity I thought. I'll persuade Mother to take David, then she'll see me acting in the play and meet all my friends. I tried for ages to coax her, but she was resolute-

"I don't like plays. I don't want to go," she said.

"All my friends' families are going. I want you to be there," I pleaded. But she wouldn't be swayed and I knew she wouldn't change her mind. I was terribly disappointed. If only Aunty Milly was around she would want to go, but since the fuss about Aunty Milly sending Dad parcels, Mother wouldn't allow her to see us anymore. I related the situation to Grandma Phillips.

"Your Mother should go. I can't understand her half the time," she said shaking her head. She knew how hurt I felt. Granddad was listening in the background and, much to my surprise, said "Give me the tickets Dolly. I'd love to see you in a play." He sounded genuinely interested. I was delighted! He said he'd take one of his friends with him. I knew Grandma wouldn't go. She hardly went anywhere, except to local shops.

Every one of us in the play got into an awful state before the curtain went up. We all imagined we'd forget our lines! But once on the stage, our nerves disappeared and we enjoyed the applause and laughs we received. Most important of all, the judges decided our play was the best of the group and awarded us first prize! The celebrations afterwards were incredible, everyone hugging and congratulating each other.

After awhile we all went onto the audience to find our families. Granddad and his friend were full of praise for us and said how much they had enjoyed themselves.

"You deserved to win. You were the best. I wouldn't have missed seeing my granddaughter in a play for the world!" he said. I was so delighted with his praise.

When I arrived home I was still on cloud nine. I couldn't stop talking about the events of the evening.

"Granddad thought the play was marvellous," I told Mother proudly. She looked bemused. "He'd say anything was good. He was probably drunk anyway!" I didn't respond to her comments as I knew it would create a row. I just wished she'd been there to share my happiness, as now I was beginning to feel dejected.

A Dot's Life by Dorothy Buchanan

Chapter Eighteen
Herbie Rides Again

One morning I awoke to find two flea bites on my arm the tell tale red discs seemed very pronounced. This happened periodically. Feeling ashamed, I assumed everyone at work would recognise them. I dreaded the comments that would be made. I tried rubbing my arm but the marks persisted. Mother was irritated by my concern.

"They're only flea bites for heaven's sake. Stop making such a fuss. Everyone gets them occasionally!" But I didn't think *anyone* at "Vincent's" would ever have them! Then Mother went in search of the offending flea armed with a glass of water. She prided herself on always being able to find and catch them.

Sure enough, she came down the stairs proudly displaying the drowned flea. "It was on your sheet. I was determined to get it." I was pleased, but it was no consolation for the marks on my arm. I decided to cover them with a bandage. Mother thought I was being very silly.

I was working with Miss Barton again that day and she never missed anything.

"What's the matter with your arm?" She asked looking concerned. I hadn't expected anyone to ask about the bandage.

"I think I must have been bitten by something?" I tried to be dismissive but she persisted.

"Let me have a look at it." She began unwrapping the bandage. I felt guilty and exposed. Miss Barton scrutinised the marks carefully. I felt dreadful, wondering how I would explain we had fleas!

"I think you've been bitten by midges." I was amazed. I thought everyone could recognise a flea bite when they saw one. I was so relieved and remained silent while she applied cream to the tell tale marks.

Although Dad had been away almost three years now, I didn't miss him at all, Mother of course missed him terribly. She didn't seem

A Dot's Life by Dorothy Buchanan

interested in anything, only writing letters to him. I tried to encourage her to read, or go to the pictures, but she wouldn't. Most of the time, she was miserable.

I spent most of my free time either at the club or Elsie's house, which at that time was buzzing with excitement. Her eldest sister Phyllis had become engaged to a Canadian and she was bringing him home to meet her parents. Elsie's Mum and Dad had gone to a lot of trouble decorating to make everywhere look nice for them. Elsie and I had never met a *Canadian*. We could hardly wait. "Herbie" he was called - even his name seemed attractive!

At last the day came when they arrived. Elsie and I weren't disappointed. Phyllis was more attractive than I'd remembered. She seemed very happy and bubbly. Herbie was all the things we'd imagined; tall dark and very handsome, laughing and joking with us in his engaging Canadian drawl, which made us both swoon. He sounded like an American film star! He kept calling Phyllis "Honey" and Elsie and I "You Guys." We thought he was wonderful.

He'd brought lots of food items we'd never tasted before; tins of Spam, sachets of instant coffee, bars of chocolate and sweets called "Lifesavers" we had a lovely time sampling everything. I spent nearly all day at Elsie's. We ate the tin of Spam and loved it - finishing it in no time! The coffee was delicious too it was "Nescafe." We'd never seen or tasted instant coffee before. The only coffee available was ground coffee, but that was expensive and hard to get. Some folks bought liquid coffee called "Camp Coffee" which was considered a luxury. Herbie told us about his home in Canada, and produced lots of photographs. They looked like places we'd seen in films.

The following day was a Bank holiday. Phyllis suggested we take Herbie on a visit to New Brighton, across the Mersey. Elsie and I were thrilled. Herbie was anxious to visit there too. As soon as I got home I told Mother all about Herbie and how wonderful he was and the amazing new things we'd tasted, and of course the trip to New Brighton. But she didn't seem impressed. I was disappointed.
    "Those Yanks are a loud mouthed lot, I've got no time for

A Dot's Life by Dorothy Buchanan

them," she said.

"Herbie isn't a yank, he's Canadian." I was hurt she should scoff about my new found hero.

"Yanks, Canadians. They're all the same," she rasped. I decided not to talk about it anymore. I knew a situation like this could end in a row, and then I wouldn't be able to go.

I was up early the next morning it was nice and sunny too, perfect for a trip to the seaside. When I arrived at Elsie's they were ready and waiting.

"I hope you guys like going on the fairground rides?" Quipped Herbie. We assured him, that we certainly did! We boarded the ferry at the Pier Head bound for New Brighton. Elsie and I listened in awe as Herbie talked in his loud Canadian drawl. Young girls on the ferry gave him admiring glances. We felt proud just to be with him!

Once in New Brighton we headed for the fair ground, Herbie bought us all candy floss, then the rides began. The Waltzers, the Big Wheel, The Caterpillar, The Ghost Train, Bumping Cars, Swing Boats - nothing seemed too much. Elsie won a teddy bear on one of the stalls. Neither of us had enjoyed an outing so much. We went to the beach and Herbie bought us ice creams and hired deck chairs. It was the first time I'd had *my own* deck chair! We paddled and played games.

Around tea time we took the deck chairs back and Herbie decided we should find a "Diner." Elsie and I had only heard the word in films. Herbie chose a grand looking cafe where we had a meal of fish, chips and thinly cut bread and butter and tea, all served by a waitress. During the meal Herbie said we should all go to a *movie* when we got back to Liverpool. All these on-going pleasures were overwhelming. It felt like a dream - it was all so magical!

Phyllis suggested we should first let my Mother know, in case we were late getting home. I thought it was the best day of my life. I'd never seen such lavish spending I thought Herbie must be very rich. I thanked him very much, but he was very casual

"Think nothing of it, it was my pleasure." I didn't want the day to end. I felt quite envious of Phyllis.

Elsie and I sat together going home on the tram. We talked and giggled non-stop about the amazing day we'd had. When we arrived at our street Phyillis suggested I go and tell Mother about the visit to the pictures, while she Herbie and Elsie waited on the corner. I ran down the street as fast as I could. I was brimming over with excitement. Mother opened the door.

"I've come back to tell you Phyllis, her husband and Elsie are taking me to the pictures in town." I gulped for breath. "So I'll be a bit late getting home. Gosh Mum, I've had a marvellous day in New Brighton." I was panting. "I think we've been on every ride. We had deck chairs each and we had our tea in a cafe. It's been amazing!" Mother gave me a stony look.

"You aren't going anywhere. You've been out all day and had quite enough pleasure for one day!" I was flabbergasted! "They have brought me back especially to tell you. They're waiting for me." Her face didn't alter. I burst into tears

"Oh please Mum, please let me go. Elsie has been out all day like me. Don't be mean Mum. They are going away soon and I'll never be able to go with them again"

"Go back and tell them you can't go." she closed the door. I ran back to Phyllis still sobbing, "Mother said I can't go" I didn't tell her what Mother had said. Phyllis looked sympathetic.

"Come on, I'll go back with you and ask her." I was relieved. I felt sure that once she saw Phyllis, she would change her mind. As soon as Mother saw Phyllis she acted differently.

"Thank you for taking Dorothy out today, but she isn't able to go to the pictures tonight. It's not convenient." Phyllis looked puzzled, but had to accept Mothers excuse, saying-

"Oh. What a pity. Never mind, we'll see you again before we go away." I was too upset to say anything. I ran past Mother up to my bedroom. I was *so* upset and angry, I screamed and shouted as many insulting remarks as I dare.

"You're always spiteful and nasty to everyone, even your own sister! You don't like anyone enjoying themselves!" I screeched. Mother followed me up the stairs.

"Just get this straight," she stormed. "You have to learn that there are more things to life than *enjoying yourself*. Everything has

A Dot's Life by Dorothy Buchanan

to be paid for one way or another, one day you'll thank me for this advice." I thought she was talking utter rubbish.

"I'm not interested in your advice. I'm just upset you spoilt a lovely day, like you always do!" Mother banged my bedroom door closed without another word. I lay there quietly sobbing in my pillow, feeling very sorry for myself. Eventually, I went to sleep.

Chapter Nineteen
Ingrid Bergman in Auntie Mary's Nightdress

I was still enjoying work and beginning to do far more in the salon. I was allowed to shampoo the clients' hair and help with tinting, perming and bleaching. I was beginning to feel quite confident. I was delighted and flattered when Mrs Vincent said she would like to teach me beauty culture too. She spent a lot of time teaching me how to give a complete facial, how to manicure and massage faces and hands.

She was very patient and spent a lot of time teaching me her skills. It took quite a few lessons with her before she allowed me to practise on the staff. I was fascinated in this work I even stayed behind an hour some evenings for more tuition! She gave me a facial often, as part of the learning procedure and taught me how to apply make-up. I could hardly believe how different I looked! Make-up, professionally applied, certainly enhanced my appearance!

I tried to encourage Mother to let me give her a facial and make up her face but she didn't like the idea at all, saying "I don't want to look a tart!" However, it was a different story when we visited Grandma Phillips. She was a very willing 'victim' and I often gave her a complete facial. She enjoyed the fuss, and each time I visited she'd say

"Do you fancy doing my face up Dolly?" If Granddad was there at the time he'd say, "You can't make a silk purse out of a sow's ear, love." But Grandma only laughed and said-

"Take no notice of the old fool. He doesn't even know the difference!"

Grandma would admire the finished result-

"I look ten years younger now. It's a pity I couldn't find a nice fancy man then I'd dump that old bugger" she'd say, laughingly.

There were lots of American soldiers stationed around Liverpool. They spent a lot of time in the city centre. They all looked very

A Dot's Life by Dorothy Buchanan

attractive in their smooth tailored uniforms. Unlike our soldiers, who had rough, ill fitting ones. The older girls at work were dating them and came to work with their gifts of nylon stockings, and chewing gum - unheard of in England at the time. I was sorry I wasn't older. Lots of girls in our street were dating them too, even the married ones who'd cried for days when their husbands had gone overseas! Mother was disgusted at their behaviour, especially when one of the married ladies gave birth to twins when her American boyfriend had moved to another camp. I remember Mrs Edge calling to tell Mother, the shocking news!

Mrs Vincent had recently come back from visiting friends in America. There was great excitement about it at work. Not many people went to such faraway places.
She'd brought back quite a few new things for the salon, including a new method of perming hair, called *"The Pin Curl Perm."* It was a much softer way of perming hair than the ones used in England. It was designed to suit casual hair styles.

At that time a film called "For Whom The Bell Tolls" was very popular, starring Ingrid Bergman. Her hair had been cut very short for the role, with soft bubbly curls all over her head. Mr Vincent suggested I would be the ideal model. I was flattered that he'd chosen me! He cut my hair one inch all over, and then permed it with the new lotions and aluminium clips, while the rest of the staff watched. The finished result did reflect Ingrid Bergman's hair. It was called "The Maria Cut" after her name in the film. It was quite unusual for the time, as most people favoured long hair. I loved it, and the attention it created!

Lots of adventurous clients decided on the change, much to Mr Vincent's delight. I had it dressed each morning, so it would look perfect to show off to the clients. The girls at the club thought my hair style a great improvement, and wanted to copy it, but no local hairdressers had taken on the style at the time.

More important things were happening anyway; our club leader, Minnie, had arranged a week's holiday for us in Wales. It would be the first holiday any of us had ever had! The boys were going to

A Dot's Life by Dorothy Buchanan

camp outside, as the hostel only catered for girls. We were all given a list of items to take; jackets, shorts, change of shoes, blouses a nightdress and toiletries. It was only costing us three pounds for the week - food included. We were all giving regular weekly amounts of money to Minnie until it was paid. Everyone was excited, and we talked of nothing else.

Clothes were my biggest worry. I had two blouses, two skirts but no jacket, shorts or suitable nightdress to take - and most of us only had one pair of shoes. I managed to borrow a pair of shorts from Louie and a jacket from Elsie. I tried to persuade Mother to buy me a nightdress but she didn't think it necessary, as I already had a pair of pyjamas (but they were so old and faded, I didn't want to take those)!

I was telling Aunty Mary about my forthcoming holiday and I mentioned my lack of a nightdress.

"I've got a new nightdress you can have" she said. I didn't know what to say as Aunty Mary was a very large lady. I thought one of her nightdresses would look like a tent on me! I didn't know what to say and just quietly thanked her, I didn't tell Mother as I knew she would think it hilarious. The next time I saw Aunty Mary she gave me a parcel.

"Here's the nightdress I promised you. I bought it by mistake." Mother was amused-

"You're giving Dorothy one of your nightdresses? That's ridiculous!" I felt sorry for Aunty Mary. As usual she didn't know how to reply. I thanked Aunty Mary and opened the parcel, and there, much to my surprise lay a pink satin nightdress - very slim fitting - not at all what I had expected! Mother was more surprised than I.

"When did you buy that?" Mother enquired.

"Never you mind," said Mary tapping her nose. I was glad she had at last given Mother a reply like that!

When we got home Mother took great delight in telling me how unsuitable she thought it was and laughed her head off when she saw it again saying.

"Fancy giving *that* to a young girl! She's got no sense at

all." She enjoyed having an excuse to criticise Aunty Mary.

I felt like a film star when I put it on. It certainly made me look curvy, glamorous and grown up! Nobody would have one like this. I just hoped the girls wouldn't think it as silly as Mother did.

Chapter Twenty
From Fairgrounds to Battlegrounds

The train pulled out of Lime Street station with all of us in very high spirits. We sang songs as loudly as we could, shared sweets and munched sandwiches for most of the journey. On arrival at Llangollan we couldn't believe the beauty of the country side. The hostel was on a hill called "Barber Hill." We had to walk across a river on stepping stones to reach it. None of us had experienced that before!

At the back of the hostel was a forest where we hoped the boys would camp, but they hadn't yet arrived. Once we had established which beds we had to occupy we changed into our shorts and blouses and took a walk around the village. Everywhere was so beautiful. It looked like a picture post-card. We loved everything. A big meal was waiting for us when we got back, which we all enjoyed immensely - corned Beef rissole and chips, followed by apple pie and custard.

We went to bed quite early that first night, although we couldn't sleep with excitement. As expected, my nightdress caused quite a stir. The girls thought it quite amazing. Some of them tried it on and paraded around the bedroom adopting sexy poses.

As we lay in our beds whispering to each other, we heard the boys arriving outside. We all rushed to the window and opened it wide. The boys were surprised and pleased our bedroom was just above where they were camping. They shone torches to our window just as I was leaning out, illuminating me in my revealing nightdress! The girls were giggling and dared me to stand on a chair, to give the boys a full view of my sexy attire, which I did - much to everyone amusement. There were wolf whistles and cheering; shouts of "Take it off." The boys threw love notes to us wrapped around pebbles. We were having great fun and making a lot of noise when one of the wardens came to complain. Fortunately she wasn't aware the boys were outside!

A Dot's Life by Dorothy Buchanan

The weather turned out to be glorious; very warm and sunny each day. We went on long walks, enjoying the lush countryside. We loved walking bare-foot on the grass. It felt like a carpet - except for the sheep droppings and cow pats! Seeing the farm animals at close hand was fascinating too. We splashed around in the river and sun-bathed. It was all wonderful. I wanted it to go on forever. We visited stately houses which we had never seen before and found them fascinating.

Flirting with the boys without supervision was a great thrill, especially when we played *"Catch a girl, kiss a girl."* They became very amorous after a few passionate kisses! Unfortunately their stay was short, as their money ran out quite quickly.
We were sorry to see them go, but soon brightened up when we heard a Fair was arriving in the village the following day. None of us had much spending money left either, but that didn't bother us.

We went to the fair and stood and watched the waltzers for awhile. Then one of the fairground fellows who was riding the waltzers called to us-
"Come on have a ride!" We all shouted-
"We haven't any money!" Elsie, Louie and I stood staring at this very attractive fellow. The others had become bored and gone off. He was tall and Spanish looking with long black curly hair and big brown eyes. He jumped off the Waltzer and strutted over to us.
"I can give one of you a free ride," he whispered. Louie and I pushed Elsie forward. He was obviously pleased it was Elsie. He told us his name was Colin and seemed very friendly.
"Stick around," he told us. "I'll be finished soon and I'll show you around." He had a soft lilting Welsh accent. This was good fun and he was so good looking too! While Elsie was on the waltzer, he was spinning it around then sitting by her and holding her very close.
"Wow, he's hot stuff," Louie said to me laughingly.

He took us a walk around the fair, he seemed to know everyone. We enjoyed lots of free rides from his friends. He told us his Father owned the fair, but we thought that a bit far-fetched. He obviously liked Elsie; we weren't surprised as most boys did, she was very attractive. They walked in front of Louie and I, he had his arm around Elsie kissing her ear and neck. Louie and I gave each other knowing glances. We both thought he was getting a bit too fresh, but Elsie didn't seem at all bothered.

We decided to stay with her for safety, although Colin gave us broad hints-

"You two can go back to the hostel if you want to?" But we ignored him.

He led us to his caravan-

"You girls want a drink?" He asked, then disappeared into the caravan, jumping out with a bottle of Cider.

"Do you like Cider?" We all nodded, although we hadn't tasted it before.

"Have a swig," he said, passing the bottle to us. Carefully wiping the top of the bottle we each had a slurp. After awhile with the bottle empty, we felt happy and giggly.

We all sat on the grass. Colin made sure he was near Elsie and began kissing her. His hands seemed to be all over her. We watched in shocked amazement! When she stood up all the buttons on her blouse were undone. Louie looked annoyed and shouted-

"Hey you're a fast worker. We don't behave like that in Liverpool. Just stop it, do you hear!" He gave her a cheeky grin and smirked

"Jealous are you?" Then within seconds he grabbed me and pushed me down, his mouth on mine and his tongue pushing into my mouth! I was stunned, excited and rather thrilled. I'd never experienced being kissed like that before, although I pretended to be angry.

"Who do you think you are!" I shouted, when I got my breath back.

"I knew you two would be jealous of me kissing Elsie," he scoffed,. Then tried to repeat the performance with Louie but she was ready for him, and kicked him hard on the shin. He let out a yell and grabbed his leg-

"You bitch," he screamed.

Elsie and I made a run towards the hostel with Louie close behind.

A Dot's Life by Dorothy Buchanan

Colin was still nursing his leg looking angry and swearing at us. It was quite dark. We were frightened, although Elsie and I couldn't stop giggling! Louie was still angry-

"Arrogant bugger, who does he think he is?" She said. We nodded in agreement, but secretly enjoyed the new experience. We told the rest of the girls about him when we got back, how handsome he was but how dangerous it all could have been. We realised the boys at the club, where really only lads.

Going home on the train, we put new words to a song from a film which starred Judy Garland called "Meet me in St. Louis" we sang-
"Meet me in Llangollan, Colin. Meet me at the fair,
Kiss me once again dear Colin. I'll be waiting there"
Each of us added further words until the song was complete, while Elsie and I gave each other knowing glances. It had been a wonderfully exciting holiday!

At last, Dad was coming home from Burma, after being there four years. I was now fifteen and David, seven. Mother was very excited and kept counting the days, although she wasn't planning anything special for him. I was disappointed. When other soldiers in our street arrived home from abroad, their families painted *"Welcome Home"* in big letters on a white sheet. Some had them hanging out of their bedroom windows or draped across the fronts of their houses. Then they had parties which would spill out into the street, with everyone drinking and laughing and getting drunk. One family carried their radiogram out into the street and played records nonstop all evening. I loved being involved in those parties. Mother thought it *very common* to behave in such a way, and as for the drinking, Mother said some people will use any excuse for a boozy night! I thought being away from home for four years, was a very valid reason for a boozy night.

The day Dad arrived home was all rather embarrassing. He gave Mother a bear hug at the front door, which she didn't seem to enjoy at all. She struggled to release herself, then pushed him into the hall, closing the door sharply. David and I observed the scene from the kitchen doorway. We were both given a quick, awkward hug, but it wasn't the emotional reunion I'd expected. This dark skinned, khaki clad man with heavy boots and a big kit bag over his shoulder, looked more like a *stranger* than the *Dad* I remembered. When he removed his cap and jacket I was saddened to see how bald he now was, and how hairy his brawny brown arms were.

"You've both grown so much, and you've got yourself a good job too." he kept saying staring at us. David was quiet and I felt awkward. I thought he looked so much older than my friends Fathers.

He sat at the living room table in silence, looking around the room while Mother prepared tea. Left alone with him, it was a strain. David and I sat staring at him not knowing what to say. Now and again he'd meet our gaze and smile. Perhaps it became difficult for him too, as he soon got up to join Mother in the kitchen.

She was busy at the cooker. We watched as he stood behind her and wrapped his arms around her. David looked embarrassed at the scene and quickly looked away.

"I can't tell you how much I have missed you, love," he began. Before he could say another word, Mother reeled around out of his reach.

"I'm not used to that sort of thing." she muttered, looking red and flustered.

"I've been away four years. Surely you've missed me?" He said jovially; but Mother busied herself and didn't reply.

There was another awkward silence as he wandered back into the living room and turned his attention to David and I.

"I'll bet you want to see the things I've brought home from Burma, don't you?" He opened the kitbag and showed us an assortment of decorative brass ornaments and leather wallets. David and I were more interested in the strange array of things he'd been issued with. We were surprised to learn they had to cook and eat from the same metal pan - called a "Dixie," and clean the brass buttons of their uniform daily by hooking them through a flat steel object so the polish didn't touch the uniform.

He seemed pleased we were asking him questions about army life and we were beginning to feel more at ease too. He gave me what I

A Dot's Life by Dorothy Buchanan

thought to be a painted leather wallet.

"This is for you. I expect you smoke now?" I was amazed to find it contained five flat cigarettes, called *Passing Clouds*! Immediately Mother rushed from the kitchen shouting-

"No, she certainly does not smoke. Fancy giving a girl of fifteen a cigarette case!" Dad looked hurt-

"I'm sorry love. It's hard to know what to give a young girl, being out of touch for so long."

After tea the gifts were looked at in more detail. Dad suggested Mother should have the first choice of the ornaments. She chose two colourful brass vases which she placed each side of the mantlepiece. The other vases were for Grandma Lawrence and Grandma Phillips, Aunty Milly, Daisy and Mary. The cigarette case was forgotten about. I was glad, I liked the idea of having a grown up cigarette case!

During the evening the atmosphere became tense again. There were long pauses in the conversation. Dad tapped his fingers nervously on the table or coughed embarrassingly. He repeated the same questions to David and I-

"Well, what have you been up to, while I've been away? I hope you've both behaved yourselves? I can't believe how you've grown." We smiled, but neither of us knew what to say. Mother was uneasy and jumpy, and kept busying herself with unnecessary jobs.

"Come and sit down love, you can do those jobs another day." He patted the chair next to his.

"Whether you're home or not, I still like to keep the place tidy," she replied in a clipped tone. A look of annoyance passed Dad's face, but he didn't say anything.

I was thankful, for once, to go to bed. It had been a tedious evening. That night I was kept awake with a dreadful row taking place in their bedroom, which backed on to mine. Dad seemed to be doing a lot of shouting. It was frightening, but I couldn't hear what it was about. I asked Mother the following morning what all the shouting was about, but she became irritated-

"It's nothing at all to do with you. It's something your Father and I have to sort out!" Unfortunately they didn't seem to sort anything out and the rows occurred frequently.

The atmosphere was tense most of the time. No happy, light-hearted moments at all. I often wished Dad was back in Burma. David became very upset and tearful. When the rows took place during the day, I would often come home from work to find him sitting on the landing in a heap crying. It was a very unhappy time for both of us.

Arriving home from work one evening, Dad met me at the front door looking *extremely fierce*, his eyes were bulging and he was trembling.

"I want the truth," he yelled, pushing his face at me. I was puzzled. I hadn't any idea what he meant.

"Where did your Mother get all this money?" He was shouting loudly now, and pushed a wad of notes under my nose.

"I don't know where the money came from," I said truthfully.

"Oh don't you? Well I do," he said sarcastically. He was shaking violently.

I pushed passed him into the house. He quickly followed and banged the front door shouting-

"Your Mother must have been *selling herself* for this sort of money, and you say you don't know? She's trying to tell me she saved it, but I wasn't born yesterday!" He snarled. I thought he'd gone mad. I began to giggle, partly in fear and mostly at the idea of *Mother selling herself!* His face became twisted and ugly he grabbed my blouse almost lifting me off the ground-

"Take that bloody smile off your face. Don't you dare laugh at me!" His anger terrified me. I stopped laughing immediately.

"This is a serious matter and I'm going to get to the bottom of it," he roared spitting the words in my face. I could hardly believe what was happening. I'd never seen anyone this angry.

Mother began screaming hysterically grabbing Dad's arm

"What have I got to do, to prove that *I did* save that money? Some women squandered their money, but I was always very careful. I thought you'd be pleased!" She wailed. Dad was red in the face. He looked as if he were capable of anything.

A Dot's Life by Dorothy Buchanan

"How on earth did you save one hundred and fifty pounds?" Mother turned to me-

"Will you tell your Father how we lived while he was away? We never had *any* luxuries or went *anywhere*. Did we? Go on tell him the truth!"

"Whatever you think, Dad. That is the truth. Some of my friend's Mothers bought lots of things on the black market, but Mother never did. We never had any extras ever!" He studied me questioningly and calmed down a little, although he was still shaking. I suddenly felt sorry for him.

"Why don't you both go and see someone to sort this out? Like the doctor or someone, and find out why you're always having rows all the time?" I knew immediately I'd said the wrong thing by the look on both their faces. They looked shocked and stunned. Dad was the first to speak-

"How dare you tell your Mother and I what to do. You cheeky little bitch!" Mother put her hand lovingly on Dad's arm and in a whimpering voice said-

"That's the sort of behaviour I've had to put up with, since you've been away." I couldn't believe what she was saying!

"Well things are going to change around here from now on love, I'll see to that!" Dad had his arm around Mother now - this time she didn't object. I couldn't understand how their row about money was now forgotten and I was now the centre of their rage.

Their arguments continued. They were now a regular occurrence. Home was a constant battle field. I tried not to make any comments during these times and spent as much time as I could out of the house or in my bedroom. Very late one night I was awakened by Mother screaming, running out of their bedroom.

"He's trying to kill me!" She screamed. I was terrified and didn't know what to do. I leapt out of bed and opened my bedroom door. I wondered if I should get someone to help, but who? Mother was lying on the floor outside her bedroom, as a steel army comb came flying through the air towards her. She screamed more loudly, as it touched her head. I knelt down beside her, I was scared, what if she was badly injured? She was clutching her head, I knelt down beside her and tried to comfort her inspecting her head for any injury, but fortunately the comb had only left a red mark. I tried my best to reassure her, but she carried on screaming in a dramatic way-

"God help me! God help me!" She kept saying. All this time, Dad stood by the bedroom door watching, as if in a trance. Angry blue veins stood out around his temples. Then to my astonishment he threw himself on the floor beside her his face touching hers saying-

"Oh I'm sorry love. I'm sorry. I didn't mean to hurt you," stroking her head. But Mother was sobbing now and asking God to help her. I couldn't understand why Mother was being so dramatic and relishing the situation. I got up and went back to my bedroom. Neither of them noticed. I couldn't sleep for quite some time. I wondered if these terrible rows would ever end.

I never told any of my friends about my home life, I doubt if they'd believe me anyway. I just wished things could be different. I dreaded witnessing any more of these confrontations.

Chapter Twenty-One
One Good Assault Leads to Another

One night I didn't arrive home until half past eleven, it wasn't my intention to stay out so late. I was usually home by ten o'clock, but an unusual situation occurred.

I was walking home from the club as usual with Frank and Billy, laughing and talking. Then, as we approached Parliament Street we heard someone moaning pitifully. We stood for a minute listening

"It's coming from up there," said Billy pointing to a side street.

"They must be hurt, whoever they are, moaning like that," said Frank as we all dashed up the street. We weren't prepared for the sight we saw. There in the gutter lay a youngish fellow, his mouth badly cut and a gash across his forehead. There was blood everywhere. He looked dreadfully ill.

"What happened mate?" Billy asked, taking out his handkerchief and pressing it on his forehead wound. With great difficulty, he told us in gasps; it took him ages to get his injured mouth around the words-

"Some gang set on me and pinched me money and said they're coming back. Please, help me get home will you? I've got to get home. I only live in Caryl Gardens!" He began moaning again.

"We'll get you home, don't you worry anymore," Billy said confidently.

He and Frank slowly lifted him to his feet but it was obvious he was incapable of walking. So they locked their arms together and made a chair lift and began carrying him.

"Hold that hankie to his head, will you, Dot? It might stop the bleeding." None of us thought of getting an ambulance or the police. Our main concern was to get him home. It took quite awhile to get to Caryl Gardens. The boys were exhausted carrying him and had to keep stopping to rest. My arm was aching holding the handkerchief to his head.

Finally we arrived at his house. His Mother and sister were horrified to see the state he was in, but very grateful to us for bringing him home. They were anxious to learn all the details of what had happened to him, and why. There was not much we could tell. They gently eased him on their settee, removed his stained clothing and quickly tended his injuries. His head was badly bruised but the gaping wound had stopped bleeding so had his mouth, but his face was badly swollen and looked very painful.

"He could have died if you lot hadn't found him," his Mother said opening her purse. "I'm going to give you something for your trouble. I haven't got much, but you're welcome to whatever I have."

"Oh no, we don't want anything at all thank you," Billy said pushing the money away. We all shook our heads in agreement.

"We'll get home now"

"You aren't going to leave here without a cup of tea though," she said putting on the kettle. "It's the least I can offer you after all you've done."

The tea was hot and sweet and very comforting. The young fellow looked much better now than when we first saw him, and insisted we all shook his hand and kept thanking us as we said goodbye.

"May God bless you all," his Mother said giving us each a hug. We all felt very proud and happy with ourselves.

It was very dark now I hadn't any idea what time it was, panic gripped me. Mother and Dad would be annoyed at me getting home at this late hour! I voiced my fears to the boys.

"Stop worrying. Wait until you tell them what happened, they'll be pleased. He could have bled to death you know, if we hadn't found him!" Billy said proudly. "Come on we'll rush you home in no time!" In spite of his assurances I felt very apprehensive.

They almost ran me home, I was breathless and trembling when I knocked on the front door, the boys shouted goodnight and I ran down the street to our front door. The events of the evening overwhelmed me. I was trembling and somehow excited too. I couldn't stop thinking of that fellow. I'd thought he was dying!

A Dot's Life by Dorothy Buchanan

I knocked on the door, I felt sure Mother and Dad would be proud of our good deed. I was dying to tell them all the happenings of the evening.

Dad opened the door. Before I could say anything he shouted

"What time do you think this is to be coming home?"

"Sorry Dad. I didn't want to be this late, but wait until I tell you what happened." I rushed passed him into the living room, where Mother sat in her nightdress, looking furious.

"First of all I'm very, very sorry to be so late, but I couldn't help it, honestly." I sat down opposite Mother. Dad stood by the door with his arms folded, he looked very angry. I quickly began explaining in breathless bursts-

"On our way home from the club we saw this man lying moaning in the gutter by Parliament Street. Some gang had beaten him up and he looked awful with blood everywhere. He pleaded with us to help him get home, so Billy, Frank and I took him to his house in Caryl Gardens. His Mother was very grateful, and-" Mother interrupted screeching-

"Do you think for one moment your Father and I are going to fall for a cock and bull story like this? You're nothing but a bare faced little liar" she spat out the words. I was dumbfounded, I knew they'd be angry at me being late, but I never thought for one moment they would disbelieve me?

"It's all true honestly!" I shouted, looking from Mother to Dad, but they remained stony faced. I was frustrated, trying again and again, even pleading with them, to believe me. But it was futile, they refused to listen. Mother looked at Dad-

"You see what I mean Cyril. I've told you, haven't I? She can conjure up lies at the drop of a hat!" She pointed her finger at me. "Your Father and I aren't putting up with any more of this behaviour from you, do you hear?" Then Dad intervened-

"Get this straight! I'm not having a daughter of mine walking the streets late at night like a prostitute, where have you *really* been? That's what I'd like to know?" He was shouting. "Did you imagine you could pull the wool over our eyes like that? You must think we're stupid!" I made lots of desperate attempts to explain things, feeling frightened of their increasing anger. But each time, I was shouted down with further accusations.

A Dot's Life by Dorothy Buchanan

"You've no idea the trouble this one has caused me," Mother continued, with her now familiar whining voice. "I didn't tell you in my letters, I didn't want to upset you. I've gone on my knees and pleaded with her to come home on time, but she ignores me. She's never been any help to me while you've been away either!"

"That's not true," I screamed, feeling hysterical now. I couldn't understand. The situation was getting completely out of hand. "You can't say that. I *did* help you a lot when Dad was away. I went messages and did the jobs Dad used to do. I even looked after David if he hurt himself, because you couldn't cope with things." My words trailed off as I saw Dad coming towards me. The look on his face terrified me. In a flash he'd removed his leather belt and cracked it across my face! I reeled and seemed to see stars. I thought my face was ripped open. It hurt dreadfully. It was bleeding too. Mother panicked immediately, pulling Dad away.

"Oh leave her Cyril." but Dad looked as if he were about to carry on!

"She's not talking about you like that and getting away with it. Not while I'm here!" he snarled. "Bloody well get to bed, and remember things are going to change around here from now on!" He pushed me into the hall. I ran up the stairs to my bedroom as fast as I could, clutching my throbbing face. I threw myself on the bed and sobbed uncontrollably for quite some time.

I wondered what my face was like. It was aching like mad. Eventually I got up and lit a candle. We used these nightly, upstairs, as we didn't have electric lights in the bedrooms. Peering in the mirror on the chest of drawers I saw it was very swollen and the buckle of the belt had cut under my eyebrow. It had stopped bleeding, but dried blood had caked around my cheek. I wished I could bathe it or put something on it to stop the pain. But I didn't chance going out of my room. Spitting on a hankie I tried my best to clean it up, then lay again on my bed still fully dressed, holding my face and feeling very sorry for myself.

So many questions raced around my head. Why, didn't they believe me? Why did they think such bad things about me? All those remarks Mother had made, saying I never helped her! How could

A Dot's Life by Dorothy Buchanan

she say that? It wasn't often I got home late. That was an exaggeration! She seemed to enjoy exaggerating every little thing I'd ever done wrong, I noticed. Why had Dad hit me with his belt? I hadn't said anything awful? That really had shocked me! I felt guilty too. Maybe I should have come straight home and not helped take that fellow home? That surely would have been wrong though? Anyway had I done that, I could have been attacked walking home on my own! My thoughts were out of control not knowing how or what to think.

A pounding headache developed and my face began to feel tight and stiff. I wished I was far away. I'd never understand either of them, and they certainly didn't understand me. Feeling terribly unhappy and desperate, I sat up on the side of my bed wondering what I should do. Get away. That made sense. They wouldn't miss me!

Everywhere was quiet. Mother and Dad must be asleep. I pulled out a dusty old cardboard case from under my chest of drawers and began stuffing it with my clothes. With no plan in mind just leaving the house, seemed the most important thing! When the case was full, I sat quietly, making sure I could hear no sound from Mother and Dad's bedroom. After awhile I slowly crept quietly down the stairs, then along the hall to the front door. When I unlocked the two heavy bolts and turned the Yale lock, just as the door was opening, I heard an unearthly roar from the stairs. Dad came charging down the stairs. I froze. I was petrified. I thought he would hit me again.

"So you want to leave home do you?" he bellowed "Well that's fine by us, just get out, we don't want you!" he wrenched the case from my hand and threw it across the road and pushed me after it, banging the front door behind me! Left on the pavement with my heart beating fast I cried and cried, feeling dejected and frightened.

In the moonlight I caught sight of my opened case with the clothes littered across the road. I got up and gathered them back into the case, but as I lifted it the clothes fell out. The side of the case had broken off. I sat on the cold step hugging the case, wondering what

I should do. I now had a violent headache. Feeling alone and exhausted I just wanted to sleep.

I sat there for quite some time shivering. Everywhere was very quiet. Then I heard the front door being quietly opened. I stood up. Now I felt cautiously relieved. I stood trembling. Mother and Dad were both in the hallway. They still looked angry and immediately began shouting again; this time saying, if my behaviour doesn't alter they will have me sent to a home for wayward girls and get the police to sort me out!

"You're out of control," Dad stormed. I was terrified and confused, wondering if it was all a nightmare. Everything was in such turmoil. They followed me, as I made my way back upstairs to bed.' Dad's voice became deafening.

"There are places for girls like you, and that's where you'll be going if we have any more trouble from you." Mother seemed in her element now relating every disagreement we'd ever had, with Dad believing everything without question. I lay on my bed drifting in and out of sleep as they continued shouting. I didn't dare reply to any of the accusations, I was far too frightened. It was the first time I'd witnessed Mother and Dad communicating with each other so amicably. They almost shouted in unison, and made it very clear that if I misbehaved again they would have me placed in a home for wayward girls!

"Just you remember you are in our control until you're twenty one!" I was numb with fear, when they finally left my room. I began to wonder if I'd imagined it all.

After the vicious rows they'd had since Dad came home from Burma, tonight they were in perfect harmony. I didn't understand any of it.

The atmosphere at home, after this episode, was difficult. Every comment I made was considered a threat to their authority, I had to be careful what I said and how I phrased it. They begrudgingly allowed me to go out after work provided it was to Elsie's. I was always glad to be out of the house.

We went to the church club of course, but I made sure I got home in good time. I was too frightened after last time. I never told any of my friends at the club or at work of the happenings at home. I wanted everyone to think ours was the happy home it appeared to be.

Chapter Twenty Two
Tea Leaves and Nylon Stockings

The club was losing a lot of its appeal now we were getting older. We wanted more than it could offer. Lots of girls we knew went to dance halls, which sounded far more exciting!

We all decided to go to a local club called "The Crocodile" it was in Princes Road and recently opened. It was called a club, but it was just a place to dance, although it wasn't licensed to serve alcohol. I had a new friend in our street, Rene. Her Mother was white and her Father Jamaican. They both worked and Rene, an only child, was on her own a lot.

She often invited me to her house. We'd amuse ourselves trying out new products of make-up and face packs. She went to college and wasn't short of anything, especially make-up and clothes. Sometimes I set her hair with a special lotion she'd bought to straighten it. She was very studious. Her ambition was to go to university. She wasn't very interested in going out with me or any other girls but enjoyed hearing of my exploits.

When I heard the girls at the club planning their outfits for the dance, I realised I hadn't anything suitable to wear and I badly wanted to look my best. When I explained my dilemma to Rene she was anxious to help-
"Come and have a look in my wardrobe. You're welcome to choose what you like." I was delighted. After trying on an assortment of dresses I chose a red shiny dress with a flowing skirt and a rose on the belt. I thought it was lovely!

The night of the dance we met at Elsie's house and spent ages making ourselves beautiful - or so we thought! We patted Nivea cream on our faces then dark face powder, brushed rouge across our cheekbones and would spit on a block of mascara to enhance our eyelashes, finishing with a red lipstick - not forgetting to add a beauty spot with a pencil! After perfecting our hair and faces we

A Dot's Life by Dorothy Buchanan

applied "Elsena" leg tan. This gave the impression we were wearing stockings. Finally we put on our dresses. We all agreed, we couldn't have looked better!

We arrived at the "Crocodile" around seven thirty feeling very excited and confident. The music met us at the door, so did a middle aged man in a dress suit who took our entrance fee and directed us to the cloak room.

"Welcome to the Crocodile," he shouted after us. We made our way to the cloakroom, where we had a final look in the mirror. The cloakroom was full of girls with the same idea. Make-up was being applied to already heavily made up faces. Some were changing clothes, some sharing a cigarette. Lots of foul language was being used too. We gave each other knowing glances. They seemed to be a rough lot. One girl standing close by gave me a nudge with her elbow and said-

"Does me arse show a lot in this skirt?" I was shocked at the question.

"Oh no," I said, not knowing what she expected. Still eyeing herself in the mirror, she continued-

"Every time I wear this skirt me mate Vera says me arse sticks out." She called across to her friend. "There you are Vera, this girl says it doesn't!" Vera gave me a foul look. We quickly moved away and decided not to bother waiting for a look in the mirror!

The dance floor was smaller than we expected only about six couples were dancing the rest stood around the floor or sat at the few tables. We stood around the floor feeling very conspicuous. The music was provided by a band of men in their forties, but it sounded alright. A young fellow crossed the floor towards us. I thought he was going to ask one of us to dance. Instead he asked a very tarty looking girl close by.

"No thanks lad," she said. "I'm sweatin'." We stood and stared amazed at such a comment. He then asked Elsie. At the same moment a fellow nudged me and inclined his head towards the dance floor. Without a word I was swept on the dance floor. He smelt strongly of sweat and had a mouthful of black teeth, his breath was foul. I couldn't wait for the music to finish.

After awhile, each of us passed one another with dance partners, none of us being very impressed judging by the faces we were pulling at each other!
Once the music stopped we grouped together at a table for a drink of lemonade, anxious to tell each other of our awful partners! We noticed most of the fellows looked similar, sporting white shirts, with the sleeves rolled up and braces, their shiny trousers appeared to belong to suits. Each had greased back hair with beads of perspiration running down their foreheads. We were disappointed. It wasn't what we'd expected.

"Let's go," said Elsie. "I think we're wasting our time here." We all agreed and got our coats. The man in the dress suit was surprised to see us leaving after only an hour and pleaded with us to stay.

"This place has only just opened. We want nice girls like you to come," he said, giving us complimentary tickets for the following week. We thanked him and said we'd think about it. Walking home we had a laugh, relating all the happenings of the short evening.

I was becoming far more confident at work. I laughed and joked with the staff and they found my description of the dance hilarious. Occasionally, I had to manicure Mr Vincent's nails which I dreaded. He was rather particular about his hands, but not particular where he put them!

When we were alone in a cubicle he always tried to stroke my thighs, which was difficult to avoid sitting so close. I didn't know what to do. I told Miss Barton and she was horrified-

"Don't you worry about it anymore. I'll sort it out," she looked annoyed.

"Please don't say anything to him will you"? I was worried in case I lost my job.

"I'm not that silly," she said. After that, each time he asked me to do his nails Miss Barton would insist she did them, saying I was too busy - which seemed to solve the situation forever.

One of the other seniors, Miss Beveridge, often amused the staff by reading tea leaves. Everyone asked her daily for a reading.

A Dot's Life by Dorothy Buchanan

Sometimes she became irritated by their persistence. This particular day was one of them. She said-

"I'm going to read Dorothy's today, because she never pesters me!" I'd never asked because I was sceptical about such things, but I thanked her all the same.

After lunch and finishing my tea I was instructed to swirl the last drop of tea at the bottom of my cup around three times and place the cup upside down on the saucer. Everyone watched as Miss Beveridge lifted the cup looking intently at the formation of the tea leaves.

"You are in for a surprise tonight," she began. "A stranger will give you something!" I tried to look impressed. She took her time peering into the cup at all angles. She looked very serious. "I can also see a dark man you'll meet in the near future, perhaps at a party. It sounded interesting, but far-fetched. "I see a lot of sharp words with people close to you." This remark made me wonder. She was about to add to this when we were interrupted by Mr Vincent. He wasn't very pleased.

"Aren't you ladies coming back to work today?" We'd all forgotten the time. It turned out to be a very busy afternoon - no time even for a tea break! I was tired and my legs were aching. I was pleased when six o'clock came.

Standing at the tram stop, I realised I'd missed my usual tram. Town was not as busy as usual. I noticed a young American serviceman carrying a box staggering towards me.

"Hi honey. 'You on your own?" He was swaying as he spoke, obviously drunk. I took a step further away from him. There was no one else around.

"Do you know what?" He slurred "My date hasn't shown up."

"I'm sorry," I muttered without looking at him, wishing the tram would come.

"There's no need to be sorry, she wasn't anything to write home about!" he grinned. At that moment I was relieved to see the tram coming. I stepped to the edge of the kerb and tried to ignore him. Just as I was about to board the tram he came up to me.

"Here, take this" he pushed the box into my arms, and

A Dot's Life by Dorothy Buchanan

went away shouting "I got that for my date, you can have it now." I boarded the tram without even saying thank you. I didn't know what to think.

I sat on the back seat eyeing the carefully wrapped box. Maybe it contained something dreadful? I quietly tried to rip the paper away, then, I saw the conductor coming. I placed it on the floor under my feet out of sight, deciding to unwrap it when I got off the tram. There were lots of people around when I got to our street; there was no way I could inspect it here.

Mother answered the door. I couldn't get in quick enough,
    "Look," I pushed the parcel under her nose. "An American soldier gave me this at the tram stop, it was for his girl but she didn't turn up."
    "Why did he give it to you then?" she sounded suspicious.
    "Probably because I was the only one there!" I replied tearing the wrapping and cautiously opening the box. I was still a bit worried, peeping inside I couldn't believe it, "Look at all these things" I shouted, shaking with excitement! There were oranges, bars of chocolate, soap, chewing gum, perfume, all the things we hadn't seen for ages! But most of all there were two pairs of nylon stockings! I'd only seen them on the girls at work! The fruit and chocolate tasted wonderful we all enjoyed it. It was such a treat especially for David! I kept the nylons, and perfume for myself.

The following day I went to work wearing my nylons and splashing the perfume everywhere. I felt very grown up. The nylons were so fine and glamorous after the thick lisle stockings most of us had to wear. The girls at work were quite envious but listened intently as I told them how I'd acquired them. Miss Beveridge was jubilant-
    "You see, my reading do came true!"
    "Of course, that's it!" Everyone agreed. But it was the first time I'd remembered her predictions.

I wondered now if I'd meet the *dark man* too?

Chapter Twenty Three
Mike, Terry and the Crocodile

The following Saturday, Elsie, Louie, Flo and I were at a loose end. None of us had enough money for the pictures. Some evenings like this we'd spend our time at Elsie's house, but tonight her Mum and Dad were staying in, so we couldn't go there.

"We've got those complimentary tickets," said Louie. "Let's try the Crocodile again." None of us were very enthusiastic. but we had nothing better to do.

"The talent might be better tonight," said Flo, jokingly. We decided to go. I rushed home to get ready, borrowing Rene's dress again. This time I took the decorative rose from the waist line and pinned it to my hair.

We'd all chosen to wear the same outfits as last time, but added necklaces or brooches. We all thought we looked very attractive and walked arm in arm towards the Crocodile club feeling quite excited. This time we arrived around eight o'clock. The same doorman welcomed us,

"Welcome to the Crocodile. Oh, it's you girls again. Glad you came back." He looked pleased.

"Let's hope there are some decent fellows here this time!" Louie said. She was often outspoken. The doorman gave a wink and grinned.

"This looks more hopeful," whispered Elsie, as we left the cloakroom. The place was full! As soon as we reached the dance floor we were asked to dance. Clammy hands gripped mine, they hadn't changed! Their conversations were the same too, with strong Liverpool accents-

"Ave yer been 'ere before?" and

"What's yer andle?" (meaning your name) were the opening remarks. We seemed to be popular, each time the music started another partner appeared, we were enjoying ourselves. Some of the fellows were good dancers and concentrated on *their* fancy steps, which suited us fine.

"Posers that's what they are," said one of my less skilled partners.

With so much dancing we were becoming hot and sticky and sat at one of the tables with a drink. It was a good place to survey the dance floor too.

"I can't see a single nice fellow here. Can any of you?" asked Elsie. We all agreed. We weren't going to meet anyone special, but as we were enjoying the dancing, we decided to stay.

We related the conversations we'd had. I mimicked the fellows I'd danced with.

"Go on Dot. What did that greasy haired fellow say to you?" Flo asked. I did exaggerated body movements and made my voice sound like his. We all had a good laugh. The spot prize dance was being announced, we didn't want to miss that. More fellows had arrived, the air was thick with cigarette smoke and there was a strong smell of beer everywhere. None of us where lucky with the spot prize.

Elsie and I sat down to have another drink, when we both noticed an unusual looking fellow sitting alone at a far end table. He wore a checked shirt, a self coloured tie, a light coloured jacket and brown corduroy trousers. His olive skin made him look Spanish or Greek and his long black curly hair hung very attractively over his forehead, he was very handsome!

"That's the first attractive man I've seen here. I could really go for him in a big way!" said Elsie

"Gosh so could I. he's gorgeous! Let's move nearer his table," I suggested. We walked casually across the floor and sat close by. Just at that moment another fellow joined our "gorgeous man" but he was quite the reverse, with sleek hair and a horrible pencil moustache. He looked older too.

"God, I don't think much of his friend though, do you?" I whispered to Elsie.

"He looks like a spiv to me," she replied. The band struck up again and we decided to dance together, hovering close to them for a better look. They both left the table and were making their way towards us. We were both blushing now.

A Dot's Life by Dorothy Buchanan

"I hope we didn't look too obvious?" Elsie whispered. The friend approached me "Excuse me," he said. "I hope you don't mind but I'd like to dance with your friend," then quickly swept Elsie away. He was polite and quietly spoken. Not as I'd imagined at all. For a few seconds I stood alone on the dance floor feeling rather silly, then to my delight the gorgeous man appeared in front of me. I was thrilled.

"My friend wanted to dance with your friend, but I'm afraid I can't dance," he said in a broad Irish accent. We shuffled around treading on each others' toes. He couldn't dance a step but it didn't matter, I was pleased to be with him. Elsie floated by doing all sorts of intricate dance steps. Obviously his friend was a good dancer.

"Now, what would your name be?" Such a simple question, but I savoured every word. His voice was rich and deep. I felt myself swooning.

"Dorothy, but most people call me Dot. And what's your name?" I asked.

"See if you can guess," he teased.

"Oh, it's probably Mike or Pat," I said laughing

"Right first time! You're clever as well as beautiful!" I didn't know how to reply. *"Beautiful"* nobody had ever said that to me before. I felt a tingle go through my spine. I thought he was wonderful. The music stopped. He thanked me and walked back to his seat.

Elsie and I rushed to the cloakroom-

"Well?" She said. "What's he like? What's his name?"

"Mike," I said." And he's *really* lovely, you should hear the way he talks." I was in starry eyed.

"I know he's good looking, but what's he like? Elsie sounded irritated.

"He didn't say much really. Anyway what's his friend like?

"His name's Terry. He's a fantastic dancer. Did you see the steps we were doing? I still prefer his friend though. Come on, you must have found out something about him?" Elsie persisted.

"I've told you, he didn't say much. Anyway keep your eyes off him I've fallen for him." Elsie smiled and shrugged her shoulders and said

"Let's have another dance together before it finishes." Once we were on the floor Terry and Mike made their way towards us again. I expected Mike to ask me to dance again but this time he asked Elsie. I was left with Terry. I felt jealous, but I tried not to show it.

"Your name's Terry I believe?" I shouted, as we danced near the band. He nodded.

"My friend doesn't like dancing much, he did me a favour coming here tonight."

"What does he like then?" I was anxious to learn all I could about him. "Oh, he's more into other things," was all he said, which puzzled me.

"What sort of other things?" I tried to keep the conversation focused on Mike, but Terry ignored me and talked about his love of dancing.

"I used to go regularly, but I have other commitments now"

"Are you married then? I asked accusingly. "As a matter of fact I am," he surprised me with his honesty. I pulled away from him for a moment.

"Well, you've got a cheek out dancing, while your wife is at home!"

"It's not like that." He looked serious. *It never is, I thought.* I asked him if Mike was also married?

"Mike?" He looked puzzled. "Yes, Mike, your friend" I insisted.

"Oh, no. He's not married." That was a relief. He looked amused. Then he concentrated on his dancing until the music finished. I couldn't wait to tell Elsie the news, but she was neither surprised or interested.

We caught up with Louie and Flo, who were just leaving. They had further to walk home than us. When Elsie and I got outside we were surprised and pleased to see Mike and Terry waiting. After a quick chat they said they would walk us home. Terry it seemed, lived near the Dock Road, further on than Elsie's, and Mike lived in Stoneycroft - he could get a tram at the end of our street! We were both pleased and relieved. It was always frightening walking home alone, and I was thrilled the way things had worked out.

A Dot's Life by Dorothy Buchanan

The one to one situation seemed a bit awkward after the loud dance hall atmosphere. I was anxious to start some conversation.

"Your friend Terry told me he's married. What is he doing going to dances without his wife?" I demanded. There was a pause then Mike replied rather sharply,

"His wife is dying of T.B. and it was she who persuaded me to go with him as he loves dancing and never gets the opportunity now."

"Really?" I sounded cynical.

"Yes. 'Poppy's' a lovely girl. She has to spend most of her time in bed. Terry's Mother looks after her and their little girl Judy. Sadly there is no hope for her, and she's fully aware of her condition, but she is very brave. I admire her very much."

"He's got a little girl too?" I was shocked.

"Don't sound so puritanical. Terry and Poppy are a very happy couple, he spends most of his time looking after her. The reason he went to the dance was to have a break, and as I said it was Poppy's idea!"

I wasn't enjoying our conversation but I was falling in love with his deep voice and Irish accent. I didn't know what to say, he carried on

"He's tried every cure possible for her without success. I have a friend who is a doctor and he's treating her at the moment." I listened intently. *He had a friend who is a doctor?* I had never met anyone who had *a doctor* as a friend?

He then changed the subject and asked me what sort of work I did, but he didn't seem impressed, when I told him.

"Where do you work?" I asked.

"I'm doing a course at Manchester University," he said casually. Of course I thought, he's a typical student with his long hair and unusual clothes and so full of confidence.

"I share a flat in Stoneycroft with a friend." A flat! I couldn't believe it. No fellows I knew had their own flats!

"How old are you?" I was determined to find out all I could.

"Twenty Three," he said. God, I thought, he's much older than I imagined!

"And you?"

"I'm sixteen in January." He smiled-

"You're just a little girl." I felt flattered at this, but didn't know why. He asked me what I liked reading. I hadn't read a book since I left school! He said it was important to read and promised to lend me some books. I told him I sometimes thought of looking for another job, and he replied.

"As Bacon once said: *'There is no fun like work'*" which baffled me.

He seemed so knowledgeable. I observed everything about him and admired his dark curly hair, straight nose, small, even teeth and flawless olive skin. I loved everything about him! We soon reached our house - it wasn't far from the Crocodile. I stood leaning on the gate, trying to look irresistible, waiting for him to kiss me goodnight like the boys from the club did, wondering what it would be like.

"Thank you for seeing me home," I said

"Think nothing of it," he patted me on the shoulder. "Goodnight, I'll probably see you at the Crocodile next week and I'll bring you some books to read." He turned around and quickly walked away. *No kiss not even a hug?* I felt let down, but very excited, I'd never met anyone like him before. He was certainly the man of my dreams!

I thought of him for most of the week, and told all the girls at work about him. Miss Beveridge was very interested.

"I told you you'd meet a dark man didn't I?"

I could hardly wait for Saturday!

Chapter Twenty Four
A Handbag, but not Crocodile

Work at Vincent's was getting tedious; I was still treated as a junior although I was doing lots more facials and manicures each day (which I preferred to hairdressing). My wages hadn't increased much either.

I decided to scan the Liverpool Echo; there were usually a couple of pages of situations vacant. I hoped to find a job as a Beautician rather than a hairdresser. I didn't mention it to Mother or Dad. I knew they wouldn't approve. Once before I had talked about looking for another job and it ended in an argument. I mentioned my plan to Miss Beveridge at work. I knew she would give me advice. Ever since she'd read my tea leaves she'd been helpful and friendly.

"You're doing the right thing, Dorothy. You have to move away from the place you trained at, or they will always treat you as a junior!" I hadn't realised that. I was glad of her advice.

I was amazed to find a vacancy for a Beautician in the Echo the following night. It was in the hairdressing department at Owen Owens' - a large department store in Clayton Square in the city centre.

As soon as I got a free minute at work the following day, I rang the store and arranged an interview during my lunch hour. I dreaded the interview. I began to doubt myself and wondered if I was ready to take on the job.

I arrived in good time and proceeded to the personnel department on the fifth floor. I filled in the usual application form, then saw the personnel manager - a very severe looking lady called Miss Kane. Her black suit and white crisp blouse looked very neat, but her black hair was snatched from her thin face into a bun which gave her a hard appearance. Throughout the interview she was cold and aloof, I tried my best to reply to all her questions politely and smiled a lot, but her expression didn't seem to alter. I was convinced I didn't have a chance of the job. She then suggested I go to the hairdressing department for an interview with the manageress, a Miss Gill. I'd never seen such a large hairdressing salon. It was very impressive.

I was ushered into a small office. A rather glamorous middle-aged lady sat waiting for me. She was very pleasant and sat chatting to me for awhile. But when she asked me if I had any experience in waxing, electrical massage and eyebrow shaping, I realised how limited my experience really was! She explained about holiday's and wages which were double what I was currently getting. This would have been the perfect job! I felt terribly disappointed. I told her I had only been taught basic facials and manicures She just nodded and I wasn't sure if she'd understood me.

After a lengthy chat she asked me to wait in the lounge while she made a phone call. I couldn't think why. I was keeping a watchful eye on the clock - I only had fifteen minutes of my lunch hour left! Within a few seconds she popped her head around the door,

"Will you come back into my office Miss Lawrence" I went in and sat down. She continued-

"I've had a further chat with the personnel manager and she, like me, thinks you'll be most suitable for the job." I was flabbergasted! All sorts of thoughts flashed through my mind. Miss Kane hadn't given me that impression. I'd never be able to do the work anyway.

"Oh thank you very much. I'd love to have the job, but I wouldn't be able to do any of the things you mentioned." She smiled broadly.

"I'm sorry. I should have told you earlier; we always send our beauticians to London for training whatever their previous experience" *London*. I couldn't believe it. I wouldn't be able to afford that! My heart was beating fast. I sat with my mouth gaping, I no longer heard what she was saying. It felt like a dream.

"You go back to work and give them your weeks' notice. I will expect you to begin here in two weeks time," she said pushing the acceptance form across to me. "By the way we supply you with overalls, and there is an excellent canteen for the staff. Meanwhile I

A Dot's Life by Dorothy Buchanan

shall arrange your weeks stay in London. I don't know when that will be yet." I stood up ready to go then thought about the cost to London-

"Miss Gill, I don't think I will be able to afford to go to London." My voice was faltering. Miss Gill threw her arms in the air.

"Oh I am sorry, I thought you would realise, we pay all your expenses; fares, hotel, food, training, all you have to provide is your spending money. So don't you worry about a thing." This was more than I had ever expected. It was all so marvellous. London, and everything paid for. Nobody I knew had ever been there. Everything she'd told me echoed in my ears. I felt I would burst with excitement!

Mr. Vincent was more supportive than I thought.

"We all have to move on to further our careers," he said. Everyone at work congratulated me, saying how lucky I'd been. I felt on top of the world.

I dashed home from work that night, anxious to tell Mother and Dad my wonderful news.

"I hope you know what you're doing? You can't go chopping and changing jobs all your life" Mother said. I thought she'd be as thrilled as I was.

"Mother, it's more money and I'll get commission on what I sell and more holidays with pay. They supply overalls too. Everyone at work thinks it's a great opportunity and they are sending me to London for training!" Mother looked thoughtful.

"You've been very lucky you know" I was pleased. I thought she'd changed her mind.

"Yes I know, I'm thrilled to bits," I said grinning broadly.

"Not many parents allow their daughters to choose a job with small wages. But your Dad and I were willing to make sacrifices for you. Anyway, now you'll be able to pay us back a bit, won't she Cyril?" Dad grunted as he read the paper. He hadn't made any comments although he must have heard everything. I was desperate to talk about everything, and get their approval.

"What do you think of them paying for me to train in London Dad? Isn't that marvellous?" Dad looked up.

A Dot's Life by Dorothy Buchanan

"You'll have to watch yourself there, London is full of crooks." he returned to his paper. I was saddened that Mother and Dad didn't share my excitement like everyone at work had done. I thought they'd be proud of me. I wondered what Mike would think of my good news. I could hardly wait for Saturday.

When Saturday came I was devastated, the girls weren't able to go to the Crocodile, and I wouldn't go on my own. I stayed in all evening feeling very miserable; wondering if Mike would be there and what he would think. I spent the evening trying to sort out some of my clothes in readiness for the London trip, but nothing seemed suitable. I'd have to ask Elsie to lend me some of hers. I began to have doubts about the job and hoped I'd made the right decision. The thought bothered me. Mother and Dad didn't seem very impressed. I wished so much I could have talked to them about it all.

The staff at Vincent's bought me a lovely brown leather handbag as a leaving present and Miss Barton brought in some cakes. They all wished me well. I had to make a little speech of thanks, which was quite unnerving. But I was delighted, I didn't expect a gift!

Chapter Twenty Five
Milly's Secret and Another world

My first day at "Owen Owens" eliminated all the doubts I'd had. When I arrived and before the store opened, Miss Gill called all the staff into the lounge to introduce me. There were twenty ladies and girls in all. I was sure I'd never remember all their names. They were all friendly and helpful. The day went well. I was issued with two lovely sky-blue poplin overalls with chrome buttons, which would be laundered for me each week. My cubicle was amazing. The walls and carpet were a delicate shade of blue and it was lavishly equipped.

A large couch stood in the centre of the room draped in the white sheets and with an overhead light. A table at the side had an abundance of pink jars and bottles containing every conceivable cream and lotion, and a large palette of make-up (all with the name of "Rose Laird" -an exclusive American Beauty house). There was a gleaming, chrome manicure table with "Peggy Sage" on the bottles of nail varnish. I realised now how sparse everything had been in Vincent's.

I didn't have any appointments booked thank goodness! Miss Gill said she would prefer me to familiarise myself with everything for a week. My surname had to be changed immediately, as someone else in the store had the surname of Lawrence. I adopted the name "Lacey," on Miss Gill's advice. "It will be easy for your future clients to remember," she said. I rather liked it.

"Miss Lacey," Miss Gill called me just as I was leaving. (It sounded strange being called Miss Lacey) "I hope you've enjoyed your first day with us?" She was smiling broadly. "I'm sure you'll fit in very well with everyone. By the way, would you be willing to go to London next week?" I felt a wave of panic. London, next week? I didn't know what to say. "Apparently, Madam Rose Laird will be in London next week and I would like you to have the advantage of being trained by her personally." I replied in almost a whisper.

A Dot's Life by Dorothy Buchanan

"Oh yes, that will be fine and thank you very much." Miss Gill was so casual, quite unaware how her words thrilled me! *London!* The more I thought about it, the more my stomach churned. *Madam Rose Laird*, I didn't even think there was such a person. I thought it was just a name the company used. Walking home that night, I felt important and fortunate. I *had* made the right decision after all!

All the girls at the club were surprised at my news.
"Don't forget to bring us something back from London!" they said. "You lucky devil!"

I hadn't seen Aunty Milly for a long time. She would have been very interested in my new job. I missed her, but she still wasn't allowed to see us, although Dad did tell me Grandma was ill and Aunty Milly had to give up her shop to look after her. I would have liked to have visited them but Mother would have been furious, so I never asked. When Dad came home from Burma, he began visiting Grandma and Aunty Milly again. I don't know how often an he never mentioned them to David or I.

One day he arrived home later than usual. Mother was getting worried. He came in looking very upset, saying Grandma had died, but he didn't go into any details. I felt very sad and again wished I could go and see Aunty Milly. Mother made no comment about her death, except to say
"It was expected, wasn't it"
I told Dad I was sorry but didn't ask any questions, I could sense a lot of tension in the air. Dad took a day off work to attend the funeral. Mother told him she wouldn't be going. I watched Dad adjusting his black tie, glancing nervously in the mirror a few times. I wanted to say something to him, but he seemed deep in thought, then, with a resigned shrug, he left the house. Mother came out of the kitchen.
"Oh he's gone then?" she was surprised "I didn't hear him shout goodbye?" She sounded irritated. I assured her he did, which she accepted.

He arrived home late in the evening. Mother wasn't pleased.

A Dot's Life by Dorothy Buchanan

"The funeral must have been was over hours ago. Where have you been until now?"
Instead of being terribly sad as I had expected, Dad looked very angry and without a glance to David or I went into the kitchen with Mother following. They were talking in hushed tones although Mother raised her voice a few times repeating,

"She has no rights, whatsoever!" I guessed it must be Aunty Milly they were talking about, I wondered what on earth had happened? I went into the kitchen and the talking stopped immediately. Curiosity got the better of me.

"What's happened Dad," I asked tentatively. "Why are you so upset?" I didn't use the word angry, although he was. His face twisted.

"I'll tell you why. Our Milly has just told me she's selling the house and my Mothers furniture, then, clearing off to live with that no good husband of hers in Ireland." I didn't think I'd heard properly.

"*Husband!* What are you talking about Dad?" I'd never seen any husband and Aunty Milly certainly didn't talk about one.

"There's a lot you don't know about your Aunty Milly," he said knowingly. "She's caused a lot of heartache in her time."

"But Dad," I pleaded. I badly wanted to tell him how kind she'd always been to us while he was away. He continued ignoring me, his anger increasing.

"Milly brought shame on our family when she was young. You didn't know that did you?" He pointed his finger threateningly at me. "She met this *no good Irish fellow* when she was in her teens. All the family warned her about him, but she took no notice. Then she found she was having a baby. The news nearly killed my poor mother! Fortunately our Reg being a chemist, helped her get rid of it. Then the soft fool went and married the *no good Irish fellow - in a Catholic Church as well!*" He'd hardly paused for breath. His anger became more frightening "My poor Mother was ill for months after that! But they never set up home together. Oh no, he had no money for that. He scarpered back to Ireland and she lived at home. We all thought that was the end of it! Now she tells me she's going to live with him *in Ireland*"

I felt completely astounded! She had a husband and I never thought she was even married. There was something rather romantic about it too. I wanted to ask so many questions but I knew I couldn't.

"Are you angry because she's going to live with him?" I asked.

"Of course I am," he snapped. "I'm annoyed she's selling my Mothers furniture to finance that layabout. She has no bloody rights to it, she bought the house; that's hers. But not the furniture! I've a good mind to go and smash the lot up!"

After all these years I couldn't understand why he had such hatred for this man and his own sister? She had looked after her Mother all her life. It was expected of her, although her three brothers had all left home and married!

"Maybe if you told Aunty Milly how you feel about the furniture she would come to some arrangement with you?" Mother quickly chipped in.

"Your Father wouldn't lower himself to ask her for anything, would you Cyril?"

"I certainly wouldn't! From now on, I've washed my hands of her! He sat at the table and said "I'll have my tea now Maud" the conversation was closed.

I didn't mention Aunty Milly again, but I was determined to find her, I wanted to hear her side of the story. Little did I realise at the time, it would take me quite a few years.

I spent the rest of the week thinking about London and wondering what I would need, I had no idea what to expect. Elsie kindly lent me brown high heeled shoes to match my brown handbag and a suit and blouse. The tattered case Dad had thrown in the street, had been patched up and I spent hours polishing it!

I was to travel to London on Sunday morning, Miss Gill had given me my train tickets, a map of London and twenty pounds to spend on meals. I'd never had so much money. I was to stay for the week in a boarding house in Baker Street, London. I didn't tell Mother or Dad how much money I had been allocated just for food. I was frightened in case they would take it from me! They didn't say much about the trip. Each time I went into details they would shut me up

A Dot's Life by Dorothy Buchanan

by saying. "Just you watch yourself while you're there and keep your wits about you." Neither of them were impressed at the prospect of my visit. The girls at work were thrilled for me. Some who had visited London gave me instructions as to how to get to different places of interest. My excitement was mounting as the days passed.

Mother promised to wake me up the Sunday morning of my departure at seven o'clock, as I didn't have a watch or clock. I hardly slept a wink on Saturday night I worried in case Mother overslept. I worried I might not find Baker Street. My thoughts raced around erratically! At last it was getting light and I decided to get up. When I got downstairs it was only five thirty!

I carefully washed, made up my face and spent time arranging my hair. I admired my reflection. I was so pleased Elsie had lent me her suit and high heeled shoes. I felt much more grown up in them, although they pinched my little toe. I'd put up with that. *You have to suffer to be beautiful,* Miss Beveridge used to say!

Mother eventually called me. She was surprised to hear me reply from downstairs. I left the slumbering house at eight o'clock and caught a tram to Lime Street station. I sat around the station waiting for the London Train to come in, watching so many people coming and going. I had no idea a station would be so busy at that time of the morning.

The London train pulled out promptly at ten o'clock, I could hardly contain my excitement my heart was thumping and my hands were sweaty. I felt I was going on an adventure of a lifetime! I put my case on the roof-rack. It looked so tiny next to the large expensive looking suitcases. I kept my handbag and beauty box, Miss Gill had lent me, on my knee. I'd managed to get a window seat. I gazed out, not seeing anything. My thoughts were concentrated on the week ahead.

The carriage was full. Most people began reading books and magazines. I closed my eyes and tried to visualise what everything would be like. I must have dozed off, as I awoke with a start. The train had reached Stafford! I felt sleep-dribble running from the side of my mouth and hoped that nobody had noticed. I felt very embarrassed, although nobody seemed to be looking. I felt hungry too, and decided to eat what Mother had left for me. I propped up the big instruction folder so I could hide behind it while I ate my cheese and pickle sandwiches.

It was late afternoon when I reached London. I'd never seen so many people rushing around. Everyone seemed in such a hurry. The streets were broad and the buildings looked huge. I found Baker Street quite easily; I'd consulted the map so many times. I was relieved I didn't get lost.

An elderly lady opened the boarding house door and led me to my room. In monotonous tones she said, "Here is the keys to your room and the front door. Breakfast is served between seven thirty and eight thirty in the dining room downstairs. The bathroom is at the end of the corridor." And then she was gone.

I sat down on the bed. It was quite a small room with heavy dark furniture, but it did have a wash-basin and an alarm clock on the bedside table. I was thankful for that, with not having a watch. I opened the wardrobe - the aroma of pipe smoke hit me and to my amazement it was full of men's clothing! I closed it immediately. It alarmed me seeing some unknown man's clothes there. I decided not to use it. I unpacked my things, carefully hanging the suit and blouse behind the door for the next day.

Hunger gripped me again and I knew I would have to get something to eat; but where and how? Suddenly I felt very alone and sad and had a cry to myself. Still feeling anxious I tried to tell myself to stop being so silly and go out and explore the area. Although I had enough money to eat in a cafe, I couldn't cope with that - I'd never been to a cafe on my own. I'd find somewhere that sold sandwiches and take them back to my room. That seemed the best option.

It was now early evening and there were so many people everywhere, which I found comforting. I passed numerous cafes, restaurants and shops, until, at last, I found a Milk Bar. I bought

A Dot's Life by Dorothy Buchanan

some delicious looking ham salad sandwiches and a bottle of milk. They seemed very expensive, but it was a momentous occasion and I had enough money which in itself felt good! I found my way back to the boarding house which was a relief. Opening the doors with keys gave me a thrill too! I wasn't allowed a front door key at home.

"When you're twenty one you get the key of the door," Mother and Dad said.

My confidence was growing with each new experience. I enjoyed the sandwiches and drank all the milk. It was going to be a wonderful week! I set the alarm clock for seven o'clock, had a good wash in the hand basin, put some pin curls in my hair and made sure my clothes were ready to put on the next morning. Then I went to sleep.

The following morning I awoke before the alarm. I'd slept well. I took ages with my make-up. I'd almost forgotten about breakfast! When I reached the dining room, four other people were already eating at a large long table. I sat down and wondered how you order your breakfast. I sat feeling embarrassed for quite some time then a young studious looking fellow, sitting opposite, surveyed me over his glasses.

"You have to help yourself," he whispered, pointing to the sideboard. I thanked him and quietly made my way to there to find an array of food under hot plates; kippers, bacon, eggs, sausages, and toast. I piled bacon and egg on my plate with a round of toast. I poured a cup of tea (as I thought) but it turned out to be coffee - the jugs looked the same but it didn't matter. Nobody else spoke to me, I was grateful for that, the breakfast was the best I'd ever tasted, and the luxury of having such choices amazed me!

I took the tube to Park Lane. I was pleased to find the tube system easy to follow, but the amount of people everywhere continued to surprise me. Grosvenor House Hotel looked like a palace! I dreaded going in and hovered outside awhile beginning to feel very nervous. Beads of sweat collected on my top lip. Taking deep breaths, I forced myself to totter through the swing doors in my unfamiliar high heels.

A Dot's Life by Dorothy Buchanan

The reception area was breathtaking; a large chandelier sparkled, thick red carpet covered every floor space, there were white marble pillars and large mirrors edged with gold. I had never seen such a beautiful place! Lots of people were milling around the reception desk and wafts of expensive perfume floated through the air. I explained to the receptionist I was on the course with Madam Laird.

"Take the lift to suite 304," she instructed. A uniformed bell boy winked at me as I entered the lift. I think he guessed how nervous I was. I winked back. I knocked on the white door with its gold numbers. It was quickly opened by a lady in maid's uniform who ushered me into a large, elaborate suite in the same red and gold as the foyer.

Lots of other girls had arrived. Most seem to be in their early twenties. I was obviously the youngest. I was given a cup of coffee in a tiny white china cup and saucer decorated with gold rings and a white napkin. A trolley close by had an array of tiny cakes and biscuits which the maid served to us. Then Madam Laird entered the room. She stood in the doorway looking very imposing. There was a quiet gasp from us all. She was older than I expected; a tall attractive lady, with thick shining auburn hair that was cut and styled very professionally. Her make-up was *exceptional*, her skin looked like that of a young girl and her colourful expensive outfit was perfection. I'd never seen an older lady looking so up to date and glamorous. I was very impressed. Her attitude and American accent made her sound so young and fresh too.

She began by telling us *where* and *how* her products were made, which included a film presentation. I made lots of notes. I was determined to learn as much as I could. Marigold skin tonic, Pat-a-creme foundation, every product was passed around to touch and smell. I thoroughly enjoyed myself having never before been part of such an event.

Madam Laird ordered lunch for all ten of us and we made our way to the main restaurant. I was horrified to see the array of cutlery and wine glasses. I'd never had a meal in such surroundings before. I didn't know which cutlery to use. I fiddled with my napkins biding my time to see what everyone else would do.

A Dot's Life by Dorothy Buchanan

The starters were served in scallop shells with a selection of sea fish I had never tasted before - it was lovely. The main course, of roast chicken, was served, with lots of vegetables and salad. It was followed by an amazing choice of desserts from the sweet trolley. I'd never had a meal like it before, it was like a banquet. The wine made me feel giggly, but everyone was in high spirits. We finished the meal with coffee and chocolates. This pattern was repeated for the rest of the week; a lecture in the morning, lunch in the restaurant, then practical beauty work in the afternoon. By the end of the week I felt very blasé with the extravagance of it all.

Madam Laird proved very entertaining and charismatic. Her new methods of giving a facial were revolutionary!

"Beauty begins with the feet," she stated. I was selected to be the client, while the others watched. I lay down on the couch while she instructed me to remove my shoes. I just hoped my feet didn't smell! Then gripping my toes firmly she rotated them in a circular movement, then massaged the heel and ball of my foot. It was very relaxing. All the class had a go at emulating her technique. None of us had ever heard of such procedure before! Then we were taught neck, shoulder and facial massage, waxing, eyebrow shaping, and electrical massage.

She was adamant about us doing everything to her methods precisely, she became our mentor! We soon became sold on Rose Laird and her products. We all gasped when she told us she was seventy six years of age! I thought she was around fifty, which I thought old anyway. She was quite an amazing person.

With my new found confidence, I decided to go to a theatre before I left London. It had been easy to save my food allowance money; having had such a huge lunch each day, I bought a sandwich most evenings (on my way back to the boarding house). It was all I needed. So I could well afford a theatre ticket.

The Wyndam Theatre was running a play called *"You Never Can Tell"* by George Bernard Shaw. I'd never seen a play in a theatre before. I made my way to the Wyndam in the early evening. I admired the shop window displays and felt excited by the hustle and bustle that was everywhere. On the way I found a shop that sold souvenirs. I managed to get key rings with *"London"* written on them for each of my friends. The play was funny and although I was on my own I really enjoyed it. I bought sweets and a programme. I felt very worldly and now I could say I had seen a show in London!

The final day with Madam Laird was memorable. We all clubbed together and bought her a basket of flowers, and much to our delight, she gave us each an enormous box full of all her products and a pair of *Du-Pont nylon stockings*. Most of all I felt so proud of the large red and silver badge (to pin on my overall) which read;

*"**Miss Lacey**,*
Rose Laird Beauty Consultant"

It had been a wonderful week, one I'd never forget. I'd learnt so much. I was now looking forward to being a fully qualified Beautician!

I was a different person when I arrived in Lime Street station, very confident, even a bit arrogant with all the experiences I'd had!

Chapter Twenty Six
In Touch

When I eventually arrived home I was surprised to find a letter waiting for me, I hardly ever got letters. With a quick hello to Mother I ran to the backyard lavatory to read it. I was thrilled and excited, to find it was from Mike! He hadn't forgotten me after all. He said he was disappointed not to have seen me at the Crocodile club and hoped I would ring him the following Friday evening. He said the books he'd promised me were wearing a hole in his pocket. I thought this remark very witty. I read the letter a few times savouring every word, although I wondered why he had signed it;

Fraternally Yours,
E. G. Buchanan

I hadn't heard the word *fraternally* before and wondered what it meant. *E. G.* puzzled me even more. I liked the *"Buchanan"* it sounded refined somehow. Mother was interested to know who the letter was from. I pretended it came from a girl at work. I didn't tell her it was from an Irish fellow I'd met at a dance hall - I thought that would have been the last straw!

Later that day I went to see Elsie. I was dying to see her and tell her all about my incredible week - and receiving a letter from Mike! I was brimming over with joy as I made my way there. I began humming to myself, and I felt more like singing loudly.

Elsie listened intently as I related all the happenings of the course. She was pleased with the memento of the key ring, although none of us were allowed to have our own door keys. Much to my surprise, she said the girls had gone to the Crocodile while I was away, and had seen Mike there.

"He wanted to know where you were," she said. I was thrilled to hear this.
"Did you tell him?" I asked.
"Yes, he's really nice, isn't he? He walked me home."

Jealousy got the better of me.

"Oh really" I said, trying to sound casual. Inside I was seething with jealousy! I decided not to tell her about the letter after all.

I was worried about my first day back at work, although I'd felt confident arriving back from London. Now I had to put all I'd learnt into practice!

Miss Gill welcomed me back and I had to relate all the happenings of the week to her. She was delighted everything had gone so well.

"We're putting an advertisement in *The Echo* all this week to promote the Rose Laird treatment." She sounded excited. "It will say *Miss Lacey will be in attendance.* How do you like that?" I was flabbergasted, I never dreamt they would do that, but I was very flattered!

"We want your training to give a big boost to the department, not only with the treatments, but selling the products which is equally important. You'll get generous commission too." She'd arranged for me to have my hair styled twice a week, my nails manicured and new overalls. Everything was happening so fast I was more nervous than ever. The responsibility seemed overwhelming.

My first treatment was horrendous, I trembled and perspired trying to do everything to Madam Laird's instructions. I put so much effort into the massage I was drained, but I enjoyed doing the make up with so many selections to choose from. The client was impressed and gave me a larger tip than any I'd previously received! By the end of the days' treatments I was exhausted! Miss Gill brought me the early edition of the Echo to see the advertisement. I felt honoured, seeing my name in print - even though it wasn't my real name!

So many changes had taken place in such a short time; my hair had been tinted a chestnut colour, and styled elaborately, and my nails were painted with different colours of nail varnish, *daily!* I had new white poplin overalls with my *Rose Laird* badge displayed. A framed certificate arrived, stating that I had completed my training with

A Dot's Life by Dorothy Buchanan

Madam Laird, which took pride of place on the reception desk. My column in the appointment book was full for weeks ahead. Everything was better than I could have wished for.

Mother wasn't very happy with my new appearance.

"Those talons look as if you've dipped them in blood, and all that muck on your face, you'll have to scrape it off with trowel!" Now that my wages had increased and I was getting a lot of tips, I decided to buy myself some clothes (which I badly needed)! *Owen Owen's* gave generous discount to staff and I managed to buy a lovely soft wool coat in pale blue, a silk floral blue dress, dark blue shoes and a handbag. I could hardly wait to wear them, being the first full outfit I'd ever had. Mother thought my choice very impractical.

"That colour will show the dirt in no time. You've no idea at all," she remarked. But her comments didn't worry me. Everyone at work said the outfit would suit me, and I badly wanted to impress Mike.

At last it was Friday. I couldn't wait to ring him. I rushed from work to the nearest phone box. His deep rich voice excited me even more this time, but the conversation was short he seemed in a hurry. I was disappointed. I'd hoped for a long chat, but he asked me to meet him the following night, so that was alright. I was thrilled. This would be the first proper date I'd had!

It took me hours to make my face up. I'd had my hair styled that day and my blue outfit looked perfect. I was pleased with my efforts. When I got off the tram at Central Station, I immediately spotted Mike leaning against the wall reading a newspaper. He looked more attractive than I'd imagined. My heart began to beat faster as I approached him.

"Hello Dot," he drawled in his rich Irish accent. I was taken aback. He wasn't just attractive, he was stunningly good looking! His twinkling brown eyes surveyed me.

"You look beautiful," he said. I felt my cheeks burning, not knowing how to reply.

"Hello Mike. It's nice to see you again," I mumbled. He linked his arm in mine and held my hand. I felt sure this was going to be the start of something very special.

We walked casually towards Bold Street. The Kardomah café was our first stop. Mike said.

"Let's go in and have a coffee." This was a cafe frequented by students usually. I had never been there. The bright lights made Mike look more attractive than ever. I felt so proud to be with him. His olive skin and mop of black hair, the casual jacket and beige shirt – all enhanced him so much.

We ordered coffee and cakes. He was so mature and confident - so unlike the boys I knew. He poured my coffee and offered me a cake. I felt very special. Not knowing why.

"Come on I want to hear all about you." *That lovely accent again.* I began telling him about my trip to London for the beauty course, my family, - everything I could think of in one burst of breath. I couldn't control my nerves and excitement. He listened and looked somewhat amused. I felt a bit silly and could feel myself blushing. Finishing our coffee and cakes, I made a dash for the toilet to compose myself.

Mike was waiting for me by the door. He took my hand as we walked around town. He pointed to buildings and explained who had designed them, chatting about books, plays and films he'd enjoyed. His knowledge of so many things amazed me. I hung on every word. We laughed a lot, his humour was infectious.

Eventually we sat on a seat in St. John's gardens still holding hands. He talked about so many things—places he'd visited, hopes and dreams, the state of the world, paintings, ballet, the theatre, - the subjects were endless. I was captivated. I had never met anyone like him. I asked him why he had signed himself *E G. Buchanan* in the letter he'd sent me.

"My name is Ernest Graham but you can still call me Mike if you like. I'm going to call you Lacey, your shop name, I think it suits you." he said with a twinkling smile.

I wanted the evening to last forever it was so magical. We caught the tram to take me home, his arm around me. Reaching my front

A Dot's Life by Dorothy Buchanan

door he said

"Goodnight Lacey. I must take you to the theatre sometime. I'm sure you'd enjoy it." He hugged me and kissed me on the cheek. "I really enjoyed tonight I'll be in touch." I was disappointed. Not only was it just a peck on the cheek, but he failed to say *when* I would see him again!

It took me a long time to get to sleep. I wished I could tell someone all about this lovely man, but that had to wait until work the next day. I knew Mother or Dad wouldn't approve of me seeing anyone who was Irish, especially after all the fuss and rows that took place with Aunty Milly marrying an Irishman.

During my lunch breaks I told the girls all about Mike. They listened but didn't seem very impressed when I said we had not made any further arrangements. The week dragged on and no phone call from Mike. I began to lose heart. I had given him my work number, as we didn't have a phone; neither did any of our neighbours.

The receptionist "Amber" was always good at pretending personal phone calls were from clients. However, work was busier than usual. I had facials and manicures booked all day. I didn't have time to think about Mike.

But late on Wednesday evening just before closing time Amber came to tell me the message I'd been longing for. Mike had rang to ask if I would meet him outside the Empire theatre at 7 pm on Friday night. I was more than delighted! He hadn't forgotten. But my next thought was *what do I wear?* That night I ironed my blue dress took my blue coat out of Mothers wardrobe and hung them on a hanger behind my bedroom door so everything would be ready.

The next day I bought some strappy red shoes and a handbag to match. I arranged to have my hair coloured and styled by "Jackie," one of our top stylists, during Friday lunch time. Everything was going fine. I was so excited. My hair was now a rich chestnut colour - a girl I knew on the perfume counter gave me a sample bottle of

A Dot's Life by Dorothy Buchanan

Channel No.5 - so at least I would smell nice!

I couldn't think of anything else but seeing Mike. I'd spent ages getting ready, but I felt very confident. Mother was curious as to where I was going, but I told her I was seeing some girls from work.

I walked towards the Empire theatre and could see Mike leaning against the wall reading his paper. I felt flustered and excited, my face was going red. He was wearing an unusual Jacket; it was multi-coloured squares of dark muted greens browns and maroons he again wore a beige fine check shirt, brown corduroy trousers and very shiny brown shoes. His dark hair hung over his forehead just as I'd remembered. His eyes were sparkling as he put his hands on my shoulders and surveyed me at an arms' length

"You look absolutely lovely, even lovelier than when I saw you last." I smiled and felt like saying *don't be silly* but stopped myself. I didn't know how to address compliments.

"I've taken the liberty of getting tickets to see *La Boheme*. I hope you'll like it?"

"Oh that's fine." I tried to sound pleased but I didn't know if it was a play, an opera or what.

"Do you know the story?"

"Yes, but I forget it now," I mumbled.

"Well, I'll refresh your memory." He proceeded to explain the full story in a very easy manner. I found it more interesting than I had anticipated.

Mike's desire to show me new things and to give me new experiences might sound condescending or even pedantic, but in reality it wasn't either. Instead, it came directly from his love of life and all that was in it.

We took our seats in the stalls near the front of the stage. I had been to the Empire once before to see a variety show, but that was years ago and I was sitting in the gods! I studied the programme without reading it. This was all so new and exciting. The theatre began to fill and as I glanced around the gathering audience, they all seemed to be very posh people. Some were in evening dress! Just

A Dot's Life by Dorothy Buchanan

before the lights went low, Mike turned around and said in a surprised tone,

"Hello Shecky." I turned in his direction and saw a rather plain, fair-haired man wearing glasses.

"Lacey this is Shecky." He leaned over and gave me his hand with a somewhat cynical smile.

"Hello," he muttered

"We share a flat" Mike continued. I grinned

"How do you do? Pleased to meet you." Somehow I knew this was the wrong greeting.

The opera began. Mike took my hand and kept whispering the story to me. *La Boheme* was sad and moving but it didn't hold my attention as Mike's hand did.

During the interval we went to the bar and met Shecky again. He was taller and leaner than Mike. We sat on high stools by the bar; Mike and Shecky either side of me while I sipped my wine. Shecky talked to Mike most of the time. He didn't even look at me. He told Mike of forthcoming meetings, of going to the Fabian society, which I'd never heard of. I began to wonder if they were communists - I'd heard of *them*.

I felt left out, so I tried to involve myself in the conversation; I said

"Are you two communists? They both looked at each other and laughed.

"Not at all," Mike said. I felt silly. Shecky was still aloof. I decided I didn't like him. I was pleased to get back to our seats and hold hands again and watch *La Boheme*.

Sitting again in the Kardomah café after the opera, I asked Mike about these meeting that Shecky was talking about.

"Shecky isn't his real name; it's a name I gave him. His name is Steve. We met on our way here from Belfast, and we both had sympathy for the Cause and decided to try and find somewhere to live together which would be cheaper for us both."

"What on earth is *the Cause?* "I'd never heard of it before.

"It stands for a better world for future generations." I looked puzzled

"-You know better living standards, more equality. Hoping the workers of the world will unite against injustice"

"Does that mean you're a Labourite?" I knew all my family were all Conservative. I had no idea what either of them stood for. Mike smiled and hugged me

"Oh Lacey, you really have a lot of learning to do, but you are so young. I don't expect you to understand."

"But I want to understand, so tell me," I pleaded.

"Next time I see you I will bring you some books that will help you understand." I was more than puzzled with the whole evening; *The Cause*, the meetings, that fellow Shecky! I had hoped *I* would have been the main attraction!

After a lovely lingering kiss at the front door, Mike once again said "I'll be in touch."

Chapter Twenty Seven
The Luck of the Irish

Work was going well. Penny, the other Beautician and I were having our lunch together. I told her all about Mike. She thought he sounded lovely but, like me, she was also intrigued about the meetings he talked about.

"You'll have to ask him to explain things more fully. You've got to be careful because you don't know who he is. I should hate you to find out he was a communist or something" That remark worried me, slightly, but then Penny was much older than me. She was almost forty. I decided older people were always more suspicious and cautious about things.

At home Mother and Dad were still arguing. Some days everything seemed fine, then the next moment the situation would change. The theme was always the same - Dad accusing Mother of *entertaining men* - it used to get ridiculous. Every male was under suspicion; the milkman, the insurance man, any man in fact that happened to call at the house! With working and going out most evenings I didn't see as many rows as I once did - thank goodness.

Mother asked me why I had made such a big effort getting ready the other evening. She obviously guessed that I was meeting someone. I told her I'd had a lovely evening with Mike, and I told her about the opera. She didn't seem impressed.

"Where did you meet him?" she asked. I couldn't tell her it was at a club (she thought I was at Elsie's when we went to the club).

"Oh, Elsie introduced him to me," I lied
"Where does he live?"
"He shares a flat in Stoneycroft," I thought that would impress her.
"Shares a flat!" She looked amazed. "Why doesn't he live at home?"
"Because he comes from Ireland."
"Ireland?" She shouted. He's Irish - he'll be a catholic, I

bet!" I was surprised at the venom in her voice. I tried to explain we hadn't talked about religion; then quickly went on to tell her how lovely and kind he was.

"Well your Dad and I don't want you to be going out with Red Necks." Mother called to Dad who was in the kitchen shaving, "Did you hear this Syd?" He ran into the living room with soap on his face.

"Did you hear what your Mother said? You are not to see any Irishman, do you understand?" The veins on his forehead began to protrude, as they usually did when he was angry. Soap was dripping from his chin, like a pointed beard. He looked almost comical but I was too upset to laugh. The shouting went on:

"Look what happened when your Aunty Milly married that *low life Irishman*, all the trouble that caused!" He splutted.

"The Irish are a rough, uncouth lot; they live like pigs, believe me I know all about them!" I was close to tears,

"Dad, you haven't met him. He's not like that at all. He took me to see an opera and to a café. He has got manners, if you met him you-" Before I had chance to finish the sentence he leapt towards me, his face close to mine--

"Don't you dare ever bring him to this house, do you hear?" He was now losing his temper in a big way and I was frightened. I dashed upstairs to my bedroom. He was still shouting. I cried and cried. Why were they like this about someone they'd never met? I thought they would have been as happy as I was. A very hostile atmosphere lasted for days. I wasn't spoken to at all, except for obvious comments. I felt very unhappy, but I couldn't tell anyone. Again I thought of running away but there was nowhere to go.

Arriving home from work one evening I was delighted to see a letter for me on the hallstand. The writing on the envelope looked like Aunty Milly's. Could it be, after such a long time? I was so thrilled and excited to find that it was! I read and reread her lengthy letter.

She and Frank had bought a small house in Waterford, Southern Ireland, She was very happy; she ran a small general shop, she had hens, a goat and geese. She also grew all her own vegetables - it sounded idyllic. I thought, *I must write and ask her if I could go and visit.*

She explained and apologised for not being in touch, saying she was worried as to what my father would do - as he had threatened her with all sorts. She felt now a long time had passed, she'd take a chance. She asked me to write and tell her all about what I was doing and how David was. She said she often thought about us and she missed us.

I could hardly contain my excitement I went down stairs clutching the letter.

"Who was the letter from?" Mother asked, with a knowing look.

"It's from Aunty Milly. She seems fine," I gushed. My pleasure was short lived. My Father got up from his chair like a raging bull, thrashing around, thumping the table saying,

"That woman is no good and *never* has been." His teeth were so tightly clenched he was hissing every word. I tried to calm him down saying,

"Oh Dad don't say that about Aunty Milly. She was always good to David and I." He grabbed my arm wrenching the letter from my hand and threw it in the fire. I was horrified! It quickly burnt to a black mass. I became hysterical.

"You've no right to do that, it was my letter!" I screamed.

"Don't you speak to me like that or you'll get what's coming to you." He was trembling with rage. I ran to my bedroom and cried and cried. Now I had no address and felt I would never see her again. Life seemed to be one row after another *and it always seemed to involve me.*

I sometimes visited Grandma Phillips. She was getting to look frail, but she still had her wicked sense of fun, and much to Mothers disapproval, still called me *"Dolly"*.

"Well come on tell me all about your job," she said as soon as I walked in. Then she grinned, "and all you've been up to. While you're here you can do my face up." I got out my make up bag and proceeded to apply some face cream, powder, rouge and lipstick to her care-worn face. She loved the attention. I told her all about Mike. She was very interested, and asked me lots of questions.

"You'll have to bring him to meet me sometime. He seems a nice bloke, by what you've told me" I finished her face and she looked at herself in the old broken mirror Granddad used for shaving.

"You've done a grand job Dolly, the old fellow won't know me." Then she recited her party piece:

> *"A little bit of powder a little bit of paint;*
> *Makes a little lady look like what she ain't!"*

She rocked herself laughing just as she did when I was much younger. I loved her fun-loving spirit. Pity Mother *(her daughter!)* hadn't inherited it too.

Mike had left me a message at work to say he would be away for a couple of weeks doing a course and would see me when he gets back. I felt heartbroken. I didn't know if he was fed up with me. Perhaps it was an excuse not to see me?

Meanwhile *Owen Owen's* had begun a drama group and Miss Gill, our manageress, decided the hairdressing department should help with hair and make up for the cast. I was really excited about it. We went to the rehearsals to see what parts they were playing, to get an idea of the make up to use.

The play was a modern one which made things much easier I was dreading it being a period piece. The leading man was to be played by one of the Directors' sons who worked as a trainee manager in the store. He was very handsome and lots of girls were after him. When they heard I would be doing his make-up, they were quite envious! Being a *Directors' son* made him even more attractive to most of them.

I was a bit nervous the first time I had to apply his make up for rehearsals, but he was very chatty and appreciative of my efforts. The following morning, before the store opened, I was in my cubicle preparing it for my clients when a knock on the door surprised me - none of the staff ever knocked on each others'

A Dot's Life by Dorothy Buchanan

cubicle doors. There stood the directors son with a big box of chocolates which he thrust in my arms

"Thank you for the time and trouble you took on my face. You did a great job." He kissed me on both cheeks! I was more than amazed, and then he was gone. I dashed to the staff room to show the girls.

"Gosh I've never seen those chocolates before," said one of the girls. *Neither had I.* I opened the box and we all enjoyed the luxury chocolates.

Over the next few weeks I was busy with a lot of the cast, helping them with their make-up, so I saw a lot of "Jeremy" (which he told me to call him). At first I thought it was the name of the part he was playing. I only knew him as Mr Barkway (or the Directors' son) - but "Jeremy" sounded so posh!

I kept thinking about Mike and wondered if and when he would be in touch again. But I was so busy with this extra evening work that I didn't have much time to dwell on those thoughts.

One morning on my way to work at the tram stop a flashy motor bike came to an abrupt standstill almost at my feet. All the people waiting were as surprised as I. It was Jeremy:

"Good morning Lacey. Hop on." I only recognised his voice. He wore a tight rubber hat, huge goggles and his big gloves were gripping the controls. His bike was making a thunderous noise - up until then, I didn't know he had a bike.

I'd never been on a motor bike and felt terrified and excited; but I tried to be very casual. All the people were watching intently, as I eased myself behind him (as if I'd done it loads of times before). I wound my arms tightly around him, while my handbag hung from my elbow. I closed my eyes and pressed my face to his back as he took off at great speed. I felt as if the bike would overturn with each corner we took. I was really frightened! But almost within minutes we arrived at the staff entrance of *Owen Owen's*. I felt shaky and windblown - what an experience!

During the next few days I had quite a few rides to work with

Jeremy. I now enjoyed the exhilaration of them and lost all my fear.

I learnt a lot about Jeremy. He'd been to public school and he wasn't keen on training to be a manager even though it was expected that he follow his Father into the business. He'd had girl friends but never a serious relationship. I told him about Mike but he didn't seem bothered or interested. I must say I was flattered by the compliments he gave me, which were varied and many, although I took them with a pinch of salt.

The opening night of the play was hectic. Everyone was on edge, especially Jeremy who was dramatic at the best of times. I did my best to calm him. He said,

"Let me take you home after the show...please...I want to talk to you on my own." He sounded so theatrical.

"Ok," I said laughingly. The other girls who were helping the performance kept saying,

"Wow! Who's the lucky one!"

The show was a big success and the cast were congratulated by the management of *Owen Owen's*. We were also thanked for helping out with the make-up, and were each given a glass of champagne (which disappointed me I thought it tasted like cider). Everyone was congratulating each other. Time was moving on - I didn't want to be too late getting home, in case it caused another row. I got my coat and said my goodbye's. Jeremy was waiting by the door.

"Come on Lacey," he whispered. "I'll take you home."

"Bye everyone," he bowed.

"Well done Jeremy," the crowd yelled. "You were great!"

Jeremy was beaming with pride.

"So glad that's over," he said with a dramatic sigh.

He threw his arm around me.

"Right, now we can really get to know each other," he said, hugging me and planting numerous kisses on my face. Although I was flattered with all the attention, I also felt uncomfortable. As we walked along the centre of Liverpool's streets he kept pulling me into shop doorways saying that he thinks he's in love. He was becoming too amorous for my liking.

"I think you had a lot more champagne than you realise,"

I said. Then his mood changed.

"Don't tell me what I had!" He looked angry. I didn't feel at all at ease and quickened my pace towards my street while I tried to keep the conversation going about the play - with a lot of flattering remarks about him..

Once we reached Egerton Street I gave him a hasty goodnight;

"Thanks a lot, Jeremy. It's been a great night. See you soon, bye." I didn't stop to see his reaction.

Chapter Twenty Eight
Sugar and Spice and All Things Nice

Mike rang me at work and I was able to speak to him as the manageress was at a meeting. He said he had missed me. I was thrilled to hear his voice.

"I'll call for you on Saturday afternoon. See you then, ok?."

"Oh that's wonderful," I replied. Although hearing from Mike again was just what I wanted I worried as to how I would tell Mother and Dad that he would call at the house. I dreaded the thought of them making a scene. If that happened, would I ever see him again?

My plan was to casually mention to Mother that I had seen Mike a few times and he wanted to call to take me out. But I would have to choose my moment carefully. After a few attempts, she did listen. Then she said,

"Your Father and I are going to see Barbara and Jim on Saturday. I'm not bothered who calls, but *I don't want him in this house is that clear?*" She shouted the last words. I was delighted to hear they would be out. "Alright," I mumbled. Barbara and Jim, a married couple in their twenties, visited our house often. Jim had a car which impressed mother. I don't know how they all met. She was a very bossy, boring woman; and poor Jim had a nervous giggle which came after each sentence. They often gave me disapproving glances. I imagine I would often be the topic of their conversations.

I planned Saturday very carefully. I wanted *everything* to be perfect. I was so excited I couldn't think of anything else. I had every intention of asking mike in. Mother and Dad usually came home around seven when they visited Barbara and Jim.

I decided to buy some cakes and biscuits which I managed to hide in my bedroom under some clothes. I thought I would ask Mike into the parlour. I it was only used for David to do his homework, being the best room in the house; having a large carpet, a gas fire, a

A Dot's Life by Dorothy Buchanan

Three-piece suite, and small table.

I felt quite daring after Mother Dad and David left I watched them through the parlour window until they were out of sight. I ran into the kitchen. I was nervous and excited. I arranged the cakes and biscuits on a decorative plate, put the kettle on a low light then lit the gas fire so everything would be ready.

At last the knock I was waiting for.
"Hello. It's good to see you again," Mike said as he gave me a kiss. I quickly ushered him in the front room. *I'd forgotten how lovely he looked and smelt.*
"My Mother and Dad have gone out. "
"Oh never mind I'll have to put up with you," he joked with that mischievous smile.

We spent some time talking about things that we had done over the last week. We also spent a lot of time hugging and kissing. It was all wonderful - I felt so happy!
"I'll make you a cup of tea," I told Mike, releasing myself from the settee. I remembered I'd left the kettle on the cooker! The water had dried up but the kettle was alright thank goodness..
While waiting for the kettle to boil again, I set the tray, but couldn't find any sugar, tea or milk. These were usually in set places. I looked everywhere and realised Mother must have hidden them! She must have guessed I would invite him in for a cup of tea. I couldn't believe she would do such a thing. I felt humiliated.
"Sorry Mike, I can't make tea after all; my Mother seems to be out of tea and milk," I lied.
"Don't worry. I'll go to the dairy opposite and get some." he jumped up and ran across the road. Within minutes he was back with milk and tea.

We drank our tea without sugar, but we enjoyed the cakes and biscuits. Before we left the house I made sure the packet of tea and milk bottle were put at the bottom of the bin in the yard and everything was washed and put away. Mike realised what had happened and kept making light of the situation. Soon I was laughing too. He was *so understanding* about everything. I felt I was really in love.

Later, when I arrived home, Mother confronted me.

"Well you certainly got your eye wiped didn't you?" She looked triumphant. "I knew you'd ask that fellow in that's why I hid everything." At least she didn't know we did have tea.

"We didn't want any tea, " I mumbled.

"Let's get this straight once and for all. This is my home and *I* decide who and when I invite people here," Mother pointed her finger at me as she spat out her message.

"Ok I get the message," I said. But she carried on "While your under *this roof* you'll do as *we say*, it's a pity we didn't have a daughter like Barbara. We've just spent a lovely afternoon with her. *She* is such a sensible girl, not headstrong *like you!*" I ran upstairs to my bedroom. I knew if I didn't, it would go on and on.

I sat on my bed for quite some time thinking. I wished I could live up here! It wasn't much, but it was mine - a single bed, a chest of drawers by the window, a wooden mirror stand, and a small chair by my bed which was always laden with clothes. Because I had no wardrobe, this chair, and some hooks on the back of the door had to suffice. One of my walls was covered in pictures of film stars that I'd stuck on years ago. There was a small fire screen in front of the fireplace, although the fire was never lit. Windy nights produced a layer of soot across the lino, and getting out of bed barefoot on those mornings was awful as the soot caked the soles of your feet. Removing it was difficult, sitting on the edge of the bath with the hot water tap only producing cold water.

I was determined to still see Mike despite what Mother and Dad said. However, I made sure I didn't talk about him. I went out most nights to the church club as I only saw Mike at weekends. When the boys at the club heard I was seeing Mike they called him a *cradle snatcher* (but this was only ever said in a light-hearted manner).

Elsie and Jimmy were seeing a lot of each other and Eric continued to take me home. He wrote me poems then kissed me goodnight - but I wasn't interested in the boys now.

A Dot's Life by Dorothy Buchanan

Mother and Dad still had rows, and Dad was excessively jealous. One evening arriving home, I could hear shouting before I knocked on the door. Once inside, it continued,

"Why did you close the parlour curtains then?" He shouted. He looked like a mad man. Mothers crumpled face was red and tearful.

"I have told you over and over again, it was to keep the sun from ruining the furniture," she sobbed.

"Do you think I 'm a fool?" he yelled. "That was a *sign* to a fancy man, letting him know I was due home." He'd clenched his fists and was banging on the table.

"Honestly Cyril, how can I ever convince you I have *never* had any fancy men *ever*," she was pleading now. I couldn't imagine Mother having any fancy man it was laughable.

"Ask Dorothy. She will tell you. All through the war years I sat here every night waiting for you to come home. I never even spoke to any men,"

"I'm not talking about the *years I was away*, I'm talking about *now!*" Then turning to me he said,

"Well has your Mother been seeing men or had any men in this house?" Even though he was in terrible rage, I couldn't contain myself any longer and I laughed,

"That's stupid. As if *any men* would be interested in Mother!" The words just slipped out, I wish I'd eaten them. My Father took a grab at me and almost lifted me by my neck. He looked as if he would kill me. His eyes were bulging his face red and twisted,

"Don't you ever speak about your Mother like that again, or you'll get a good hiding. Do you understand?" I nodded. I was frightened of what he might do next.

"She's getting so impudent since she met that Irish lout," Mother switched the conversation.

"Well don't you worry love I'll soon sort her out." Dad had now softened his voice. Mother continued,

"You've no idea what I have to put up with. She never does a thing in this house; she's out *every* night and all she thinks of is *pleasure! Pleasure! Pleasure!*" My Father had moved closer to her now, his hand, on her shoulder,

"Things are going to change in this house," he said. "All

we have done for you and all *you do* is throw *dirty water in our faces."*
I felt stunned. Yet again Mother cleverly switched the focus of their anger on *me* and *their* argument was now forgotten!

I went to my bedroom. They were both at the bottom of the stairs still shouting. This situation was repeated so many times. It seemed to me that the only time they were in harmony was when I was the topic, usually instigated by Mother.

All these constant rows upset me, but I believe they upset David far more. He didn't have any escape as he wasn't allowed to play out in the street. On rare occasions, Mother would allow him to bring a friend home from school to play in the house, otherwise he would read or play a game on his own. He spent more time with Mother and Dad, than he did with children his own age. Each weekend he would go with Mother and Dad on their day trips to places like New Brighton, or Heswall (which were across the river Mersey) - then a bus ride to a seaside area. I remember what boring days they were when I had to go. But David *never* complained.

He was very bright at school and read a lot. He was interested in Astronomy and taught himself all the names of constellations and planets. Mother flaunted his cleverness to everyone; it seemed they had great hopes for his future and theirs. After tea, he would go to the parlour to do his homework until bedtime.

I still went to the church club on weekdays but Friday was the day I looked forward to most, when I would see Mike. He had told me about his family and life in Ireland. His Mother had died when he was nine and his father found life very difficult without her. Mike said that his father lost all interest in the home or family once his wife died. His sister Georgina, had left home in her teens, and Mike moved to England. His two brothers married and made their homes in Ireland.

After school, he went to college to study to be a watchmaker but then left to go into the Fleet Air Arm as a mechanic on aircrafts. His own father was a staunch protestant and when his elder brother married a catholic girl, his father disowned him. Mike said he hated

A Dot's Life by Dorothy Buchanan

the bitterness that religion brought, and didn't believe in any faith.

He'd brought me a selection of books to read on philosophy. I found them very hard to understand. Every sentence seemed to use words I had never heard of! But I desperately wanted to learn about things I had never heard of. When I told Mike, he understood and told me to forget them for now.

"Do you ever read a newspaper?" Mike asked.

"We get the *News of the World* on Sundays but I never read it." I didn't know anyone who bought a daily paper. He smiled and pulled out a paper form his pocket called *The News Chronicle*,

"This is a good daily paper, so is *The Manchester Guardian*, He flicked over the pages and pointed out articles, film guides, book and theatre revues and the editorial. "The editorial tells you what the paper believe in, so it gives you a good idea what its principles are." I had no idea what he was talking about.

"How do you mean?" I asked.

"The two papers I mentioned are what are considered left wing, that means *socialist* - and that's what I believe in."

"Does that mean you are a communist?" Suddenly I felt worried.

"Not at all, whatever gave you that idea? Socialism is very different." I was relieved. Apart from our wonderful amorous moments, his wealth of knowledge amazed me. He took me to so many places - some I never knew existed, *The Walker Art Gallery*, *The Museum*, stately homes like *Speke Hall*, *The Reference Library*, - even a walk in the park was magical he knew the names of trees, wild flowers, and birds! I had never met anyone like him, *ever*. His interests and enthusiasm rubbed off on me. I felt I had been introduced to a new way of looking at everything. I felt so happy and was sure I was in love.

Mother and Dad still didn't mention him. Neither did I, but I was itching to tell them the places I had visited.

Chapter Twenty Nine
A Last Supper

Mother went to see Grandma Phillips' a lot as she had taken ill. I often went after work. She was usually in bed and looked old and frail but she still laughed a lot. While I was there once, she asked me if I still saw that *Irish fellow*. When I told her I did, she said,

"Why don't you bring him here to meet me?"

"I'd like to very much because I can't take him home," I replied.

"Oh I know all about that Dolly. Believe me I told your Mother off when she told me about hiding the tea and sugar. I was ashamed a daughter of mine could do such a thing." I was more than pleased to hear she had spoken up on my behalf. I gave her a hug she kissed my cheek

"Thanks Gran. I *will* bring him. By the way is there anything you would like me to get for you?"

"Yes," she chuckled. "A few five pound notes, a nice bit of chicken, and a nice young man to keep me company." She still had that twinkle in her eye.

I told Mike of my conversation with Grandma, and he was looking forward to seeing her.

"Tell you what. I'll get her some roast chicken." Chicken was only eaten at Christmas. I didn't know anyone who had chicken any other time. I thought he was joking. I laughed

"How will you get roast chicken?"

"Easy- I'll buy one in town and roast it. I *can* cook you know." he looked surprised. I had never known a man who could cook anything like a chicken! I wasn't sure I believed him.

We arranged to go to Grandma's the following Saturday. Meeting Mike at the end of our street, I noticed he had a rucksack across his shoulder. I wondered what it contained - probably books which he often had with him. I didn't ask about the chicken, I thought he'd probably forgotten.

A Dot's Life by Dorothy Buchanan

We arrived at Grandma's in the afternoon,
"Come in," she called, when I tapped on her two-roomed flat door. She was in bed. Her living room looked dusty and dingy and her lined, grey face looked tiny against the propped up pillows. Her dark hair was sparse and yellow patches of skin shone through it. She greeted us with outstretched arms, which were bony and thin. I felt sad to see how much she had changed since last I saw her, but her broad smile was the same.

I introduced Mike and she gave him a handshake and pat on his cheek.
"You look a nice enough fellow to me. Put the kettle on Dolly and make us all a nice cup of tea." After putting on the kettle I proceeded to wash the mountain of dirty dishes in the sink. I could hear Grandma and Mike laughing. I was thrilled at last someone in my family had met him.
"Bring me some chuck in Dolly."
When I took the mugs of tea and Grandma's bread into the living room I was surprised to see Mike sitting on the bed and Grandma clutching a parcel in one hand and the on the bed were a small bottle of Whisky, a bunch of flowers and some sweets.
"Bring me that bread. Your Mike has brought me some chicken in here," she shouted, pointing to the parcel. Mike must have cooked the chicken that morning – just for Grandma Phillips!

Her small dark eyes were dancing. "Look! Whisky, flowers and sweets as well! You've got a good fellow, Dolly. You look after him, do you hear." with that she poured some whisky into her tea. "This is better than Christmas!" She said as she munched on the bread and chicken. I went into the kitchen to find a vase for the flowers, but I had to make do with a jam jar.
"Put the flowers on the sideboard, I can see them there." she looked *so happy* as she addressed Mike.
"I'm glad to see our Dolly has found a good fellow. If you look after her as well as you've looked after me tonight; I couldn't ask for more!"

I was thrilled that Mike had been so thoughtful. I had never known anyone make such a lovely gesture to someone they had never met.

I hadn't brought anything! I felt so proud of Mike. When we left Grandma, she was gently sleeping – her cheeks glowing.

Sadly. a few weeks later, Grandma Phillips died. I was just pleased that Mike had met her.

Granddad Phillips couldn't cope living on his own, and went to live with Aunty Mary, but it only lasted a couple of weeks. Aunty Mary said she couldn't cope with his demands. Mother wouldn't even consider having her father live with us. Sadly he had to go into an Old People's Home, and neither, my Mother or Aunty Mary, ever visited him. He died after being there only a couple of weeks.

Aunty Mary often visited us but on some occasions, Mother pretended she was out and didn't answer the door. One particular day she was allowed in and Mother seemed pleased when Aunty Mary produced a bottle of Sherry.

"Tom won two bottles in a raffle, so I thought you would like one to keep for Christmas," Aunty Mary explained.

"Thanks Mary. Cyril and I *always* buy *Harvey's Bristol Cream*, at Christmas, which is the best, but I expect *this* will come in handy. I'll put it in the kitchen to show Cyril when he gets home from work."

Chapter Thirty
Crucifixion and Burial

The atmosphere at home was still volatile.

Like so many other houses, an insurance collector called regularly -- Mr Dawson was his name. Mother usually had the money and policy book ready on the hall stand. He was never invited into the house. One day he asked if they would like to take a further Life insurance, Mother told him to call when Dad was home; a day and time was arranged. I happened to be in that day.

Mr Dawson arrived just before three o'clock, the time Dad usually got home. Mother fussed a lot, as she did with anyone official. He was given a cup of tea with a china cup and saucer. *Would you like a biscuit, Mr Dawson?* Dad arrived shortly afterwards

"Oh, hello Cyril. Mr Dawson has just come." Dad didn't reply but took off his hat and coat slowly and hung them in the hall. He didn't look at all pleased.

"Nice cup of tea Mrs Lawrence, just what the doctor ordered," Mr Dawson said in a jovial fashion.

"Oh do have another one, Mr Dawson. Have a biscuit this time!" Mother said. "And here is your cup of tea Cyril." She placed it on the table where Dad usually sat.

"Had a good day at work Mr Lawrence? 'Keeps you out of mischief. Eh!" Mr Dawson winked. Dad said nothing. Mother began telling Dad the advantages of the suggested policy.

"Anyway," she said. "Mr Dawson will explain it all to you." I hovered in the back kitchen. I sensed Dad was getting angry, he had that look. Mother continued to give Mr Dawson her full attention. Aware the atmosphere was becoming tense, Mr Dawson began making silly jokes. He looked uncomfortable, and out of nervousness he picked up the poker and began poking the fire.

"Your fire is getting low. You need more coa-" Dad ran towards him grabbing the poker from his hand,

"Who the hell do you think you are, smart-arse? Kidding

me you want a policy when all the time you're after my wife! I know *your game!* I wasn't born yesterday!" He brandished the poker at Mr Dawson who looked terrified. His head was touching the back of his chair, and as Dad leant over him, his gloves and brief case fell to the floor.

"This is not the first time he's been here, the way *you* treated him! Poking our fire! The bloody cheek of him!" Dad's anger rose again. "Get out of my house, and don't come here again you fucking bastard." I had never heard him use words like that.

"Oh no, Cyril," mother whimpered, trying to hold on to Dad's arm but he pushed her aside as he marched Mr Dawson through the hall into the street. Mother tried to sound concerned,

"Here are your gloves and brief case Mr Dawson, you'll need them!" Then Dad grabbed them from her and threw them after Mr Dawson who stumbled down the front steps. Banging the front door Dad came into the living room like a man possessed. Ranting and raving to Mother as to how right he had been all along.

"So this is your fancy man is it? I'll soon put a stop to that!" Mother kept crying and pleading.

"What have I done to deserve this," but Dad ignored her and carried on with his accusations. Then he spotted the wine bottle in the kitchen, he almost exploded with fury-

"My God! What's this? It was all arranged wasn't it? You were going to have a drink with him, but I spoilt your fun didn't I, coming home too soon? He spat out every word then rushed into the kitchen, smashing the top off the bottle of Sherry and pouring the contents down the sink. I was tempted to intervene, but I was too afraid. Mother was now kneeling in front of Dad with her hands clasped together, praying, in a whining voice, for God to help her. Dad pushed her away and she fell against the chair which caused further crying and praying, although she wasn't really hurt. I went to my bedroom and lay on the bed with a pillow over my head to blot out the shouting.

I dreaded the next day, wondering what would happen. Much to my surprise everything seemed amicable. I felt sorry for Mother as I knew she was telling the truth like so many other occasions.

"I wish Dad wouldn't row with you so much," I tried to sound understanding.

A Dot's Life by Dorothy Buchanan

"Rows?" Mother looked shocked. "*Your* Father and I have *disagreements*, every married couple have them. Anyway, it's because your Father thinks *so much of me*, I know he gets a bit jealous sometimes. But he is a good husband." she paused for a moment then went on. "When I want your opinion I'll ask for it. If your Father knew what you've just said, he'd go mad!" *She* was angry now! "I've told you before. You have too much to say. What your Father and I do or say is *our* business *not yours*. In future keep your mouth shut do you hear?" I mumbled,

"Sorry." Attempting to change the subject I began chatting about work. "We have a new cleaner in our department; a very refined sort of lady, - not at all like our usual cleaners. We were all impressed when she told us she'd never done cleaning before and only took the job to help pay her daughter's wedding. Wasn't that good of her?" Mother glanced at me and pulled a face.

"More fool her! I'd never go out cleaning to pay for a wedding." I should have anticipated that sort of reply, but I always hoped she would show some understanding.

Chapter Thirty One
High heels and Flats

I hardly ever went to the club now; I was too busy seeing Mike. He introduced me to so many things. I was reading books I never knew existed - philosophy, poetry, autobiographies - we'd spend hours discussing them. I was a willing pupil anxious to learn – especially with missing so much school during the war.

On my eighteenth birthday Mike sent me a lovely card and a bouquet of red carnations. I received birthday cards from Aunty Milly (sadly with no address) lots from work and the club gang. There were none from Mother and Dad, or David. While I was opening my cards Mother said,
      "Your father and I didn't send a card. There's no point, when you live here. We'll get you a cardigan or something instead."

That evening Mike took me for a meal, then for drinks at the Philharmonic pub in Hope Street, a very popular landmark of Liverpool, with its ornate Victorian splendour. Lots of actors, and musicians, frequented there. I thanked Mike for the flowers and he said carnations were his favourite - especially red ones. Although I enjoyed the evening I was surprised he hadn't brought me a present, apart from the lovely flowers. During the evening he asked if I would meet him at lunch time the following day.

Mike was waiting for me, as arranged, at the staff entrance. Linking my arm he rushed me to a tram stop. We boarded a tram to the other end of town, two stops away. I wondered where we were going, and why. Mike kept winking and hugging me saying it was a surprise.

We arrived at a shoe shop, not the usual type, but one which specialised in ladies hand-made shoes. There were lots of beautifully styled leather shoes displayed in the small window. I had never seen the shop before.
      "Come on, let's go in and see what they have."I was

A Dot's Life by Dorothy Buchanan

stunned. Inside were lots more shoes in glass cases around the shop. A very smart middle-aged gentleman came to greet us with a handshake

"Have a good look at all the shoes and let me know which you like and I'll make them for you." I felt quite overwhelmed. I wondered how much they would cost! Mike insisted I try on lots of different styles, and then he spotted a lovely pair of platform heeled sling backs in red; not a bright, vivid red - more of a plum colour. They had really high heels too.

"Try these on, they'll suit you." Mike held up the shoes. I put them on and walked around in them. They felt amazing! They were just what I'd always dreamed of having. I had my feet measured in every way, I kept hoping my feet didn't smell!

"They will be ready at the end of the week," the gentleman told us. I don't know how much Mike paid for them. He asked me to wait outside while he paid. I had never had such a wonderful gift. I was so thrilled. I didn't know how to thank him. I jumped up and down and hugged Mike when he came out of the shop.

"I wanted to get you something special for your birthday, because you are so special to me." We hugged and kissed again, much to the surprise of passers-by! All the girls at work thought the shoes were an unusual novel gift - "Lucky you," they said.

I was so excited I wanted to tell everyone. When I arrived home I told Mother of the eventful day I'd had.

"What's the point in having shoes made for you when you can get shoes that fit you from a shop; unless of course you have *deformed feet* or something." Mother said with a smirk.

The next time I saw Mike he asked if I'd like to go to his flat for a meal the following Sunday. I was dying to see where he lived.

"I'll make you a nice meal," he said, smiling. I didn't tell Mother or Dad I was going to Mike's flat. I knew they would try and stop me.

Mike's flat was on the ground floor of a large Victorian house in a secluded square off Derwent Road. The area was called Stoneycroft, in the suburbs of Liverpool. The square was precisely that, six large houses surrounding a grass and tree area. It looked very posh. I had no idea it would be like this.

I rang the bell, on the highly polished black front door, and only then noticed a set of bells with name plates on the side wall, but it was too late. A middle aged attractive lady answered. When I explained who I'd called to see, she pointed to the *Buchanan/ Crookes* bell.

"Sorry to disturb you," I muttered.

"Not at all, come on in, you want the first door on the left." She disappeared along the hall and down some steps.

Mike welcomed me with a hug and kiss.

"That was the landlady, Eve, who let you in," Mike explained "Sit down and I'll make you a drink." he disappeared down a flight of stairs in the corner of the room. I sat down and took a look around the room. It was all so different to what I expected. A large bright airy room with cream walls, mahogany woodwork a tiled fireplace, two easy chairs (each side of the tiled fireplace) a large settee and lots of shelves - with more books than I'd ever seen in any home! A large polished table stood between the two front windows. I loved the views too! No houses to be seen - just a lawn and big trees. There was a bed in each corner of the room. They didn't look like beds at all, no headboards just beige and brown covers and matching cushions. I was quite amazed that Mike lived in this lovely flat. I followed Mike into the kitchen which again was a surprise; black and white tiled floor, white walls and cupboards, a small table and two chairs. I could smell the aroma of curry coming from the cooker.

"I've cooked a meal for us. It will be ready soon, meanwhile, let's go and take our tea in the living room." We sat opposite each other by the fire. It was *so* cosy.

A large brown paper parcel sat on the coffee table I hadn't noticed it before

"That's *your* parcel. Why don't you open it?" Mike was grinning. I wrenched the paper off as quickly as I could. Inside was a shoe box. I shrieked with delight, here at last were my red shoes. I put then on immediately.

A Dot's Life by Dorothy Buchanan

"Oh Mike, they are wonderful! Thank you, thank you!" I rushed over to his chair and hugged and kissed him.

"They look great," Mike said. I sat looking and stroking them. They fitted *perfectly*. I felt very sophisticated. They were the best thing I'd ever had. I walked up and down the room, posing. Mike was amused at my actions. A knock came on the door.

"Come in," shouted Mike. It was the landlady.

"Sorry to disturb you, but I've just made some apple pies and I know you love them," she said with a wink.

"Thank you, Eve. By the way this is Dot." Mike stood up. She offered me a limp handshake. I disliked her. I suppose I was jealous, especially of her pies. When she left I said,

"She's very gushing isn't she," while trying to hide my jealousy. Mike smiled knowingly.

"Oh Eve is a bit flirty, but we take no notice of that. She has a hard time. Her husband was in a car crash a few years ago which left him completely blind. She cares for him very well and for her young daughter - as well as keeping this big house clean! I think she just gets a bit lonely." I felt ashamed at my jealousy.

No sooner had she gone when Steve came in. I was disappointed I'd hoped Mike and I would be on our own! Mike introduced me again,

"I know you met briefly at the theatre, but here we go again, Dot this is Steve." He politely shook my hand,

"Hello again Dot" then sat down and opened a newspaper. Mike and I continued talking and made a few attempts to bring Steve into the conversation, but he didn't appear interested. I felt uncomfortable and wondered if he was shy or rude? Mike went into the kitchen to serve the meal and I followed him.

"This looks delicious," I said. I was impressed that Mike had made this meal without much effort. The three of us sat in silence for awhile enjoying the curry, then Steve began telling Mike of some Labour party meetings. Then they had a lengthy chat which seemed to be about politics. I sat and listened, feeling a bit left out.

Steve got up after the meal and made coffee.

"Hope you like coffee?" He said looking in my direction. I nodded. That was the first and only time he'd even looked at me that afternoon. I couldn't understand why. It puzzled me. After we drank the coffee I was relieved when Mike suggested we go out for a drink. We would be alone again.

While sitting in the pub I asked Mike about Steve and mentioned how surprised I was that he hadn't spoken to me.
"Oh take no notice of Steve. He is more interested in politics than anything else. That is his life. He doesn't seem to have time for girls." I thought this very strange, but didn't say so. I had very mixed feelings about things when I got home. I loved Mike's flat, but I was surprised he shared it with a person like Steve, who in *every* way was so different. Maybe it was just a convenient arrangement, financially. I knew Mike was interested in politics but he didn't dedicate his life to it, as Steve obviously did.

I went to the flat quite a few times after that first visit; mostly we were on our own (which was lovely) and, on the occasions that Steve was there, he disappeared quickly without much chat. I still found him very odd.

Chapter Thirty Two
To Pin a Sin on Tim

Mike introduced me to a few of his friends who often called when I was at his flat. One was an elderly man called 'I.P.' I never knew his real name. He talked with Mike about things I knew nothing about; the government, world affairs, political meetings, etc., but I listened and tried to look interested. Sometimes it became a heated discussion, which I thought was a row. I was always surprised when it ended amicably.

Another of Mike's friends' was Tim. He was around forty, always fun to be with and he had a great sense of humour. I liked him very much. He wasn't interested in politics at all. Mike told me he was married with four children and had a small ice cream business. However, the factory was losing money rapidly, so he had taken a job repairing cars in a garage. He had a car, a *Hillman Minx*. Mike and Steve helped him out in a small way financially. In turn, Tim was always anxious to run us anywhere. He often took Mike and I on trips in the car, when he was off work.. I learnt that he had gone back to live with his Mother as the financial situation had caused him and his wife to separate, which was sad, as he talked so lovingly about his wife and children, whom he visited often.

He once took Mike and I to Buxton. We visited Poole's Caves, a well known tourist attraction. I found it exciting and frightening to be walking deep underground. Mike as usual, was very informative explaining the long pointed rocks on the ceiling and floor were called stalagmites and stalactites, formed by constant dripping of water. It was a lovely day trip.

Afterwards, Tim and Mike took me home in the car. Mother came to the door and noticed the car.
"You could have invited them in for a cup of tea." She said after closing the door. I couldn't believe what I was hearing! But I knew she would enjoy having a car parked outside. Not many people had cars.

A Dot's Life by Dorothy Buchanan

"Oh okay, I will, next time, thanks." She seemed interested.

"Who is this Tim, anyway?"

"He's a friend of Mikes. He often takes us on day trips."

"Oh really." She looked surprised. Perhaps it was the car that had swayed her, but whatever it was, I felt excited at the prospect of inviting Mike into our house. I thought that once they got to know him, their attitude would change.

I took full advantage of this offer; the following week Tim had called to see Mike while I was there.

"Don't worry about rushing to get the tram home. I'll run you," Tim said. It was just what I'd hoped for! I didn't tell Mike what Mother had said, in case she changed her mind. When we got to the front door, I asked them to wait a minute. I knocked on the door. Mother answered.

"Is it alright if Mike and Tim come in?" I asked, dreading she would say no.

"Yes, you can ask them in for a cup of tea." I ran to the car I was very excited.

"Would you both like to come in and have a cup of tea?" Although I knew Tim neither drank tea or coffee.

"Are you sure?" Mike looked surprised.

"Yes. Mother suggested it." I was elated. Mike had at last been invited into my home! Mother stood holding the door as she scrutinised them walking through the hall.

I introduced them watching Mothers expression, as she shook hands with Mike. I noticed she spent time looking him up and down, I hoped she would approve. She disappeared into the kitchen and I followed her.

"By the way, Tim doesn't drink tea or coffee."

"I've never heard of that before. What will he have then?" Mother said. Tim must have heard the conversation and shouted-

"A glass of water will be fine for me, thanks."

"Would you like a glass of milk, instead?"

"Oh thank you Mrs Lawrence that would be fine."

I was so pleased things were going well. Mother brought in a tray of

A Dot's Life by Dorothy Buchanan

tea and a glass of milk and even a plate of biscuits. Tim complimented Mother about the living room which pleased her very much. We all chatted about different room styles. I told her how nice Mikes flat was. I knew we were only making small talk, but thought it important that we were finding common ground. I wished Dad would hurry up and come home to complete things.

As if my wish was granted I heard Dad opening the front door. I rushed up the hall to greet him.

"Hello Dad. Mike and his friend, Tim brought me home in the car - that's it outside," I said pointing to it before he closed the front door. Dad didn't reply. He came into the living room, as Mother brought his tea. Tim and Mike stood up as I made the introductions; Dad ignored their intended handshakes and went back to the hall to hang up his coat. Both Tim and Mike looked at each other frowning, and then sat down. I felt embarrassed but tried to ignore the situation, perhaps Dad hadn't noticed their outstretched hands? With a nervous grin I offered them biscuits. They politely refused, and by now, the atmosphere felt tense. Dad came into the room looking pokerfaced. I couldn't understand why. Much to my amazement he began addressing Tim with a very angry voice.

"Who the hell are *you*?" Tim was taken aback to say the least, but in a quiet voice he replied.

"I'm a friend of Mike and Dot's." Before he could say another word Dad said.

"So Dorothy has brought you here for her Mother has she?" Tim thought it must be a joke and smiled weakly.

"I have a wife and children; I can assure you I'm not interested in anyone else." The smile had now left his face. He realised Dad was serious. Dad continued, now becoming more abusive.

"Don't give me that. Mate, I know *your* game!" Tim was by now very flustered

"I've been accused of some things in my life, but I can assure you this is something I have never been accused of. The reason I am sitting here is that Mrs Lawrence invited us in, after we had brought Dot home. I just can't believe anyone could read some other motive into that." Tim looked annoyed, but kept his control.

185

Before Dad had time to reply Mike jumped up. I'd never seen him so angry-

"Look here, Mr Lawrence. I take great exception to your ridiculous remarks. Tim kindly offered to bring Dot home in the car. Mrs Lawrence asked us in for a cup of tea - it's as simple as that." Mike and Tim got up to go. Dad shouted again. His temper was at boiling point, he spluttered out the words.

"Don't give me that cock and bull story. *That cow* has brought your friend here for her Mother!" He banged his fist on the table. "It would suit her just fine, the little bitch; you must think I was born yesterday! Get out of my house both of you. Don't dare darken my door again or you'll get what's coming to you!" They were now in the hall. I stood there feeling helpless, ashamed and stunned. As they brushed past me Mike gave a tap on my arm and whispered.

"Don't worry, see you soon."

What must they think of me? Will I ever see Mike again? Why have things gone so wrong? My thoughts were quickly interrupted. Dad pushed me into a chair in the living room, hi face, close to mine, twisted and ugly.

"Your little game hasn't worked, has it? You now have a lot of explaining to do!" I could hear the car moving away. I felt so hurt and sad and began to cry hysterically.

"Come on. I'm waiting. You thought that man would be ideal for your Mother did you? And what's this?" He pointed to the glass of milk. Why should they have Milk? Wasn't tea good enough?"

"Look Dad, you have it all wrong," I said between sobs. "Tim is married and he was just giving me a lift home with Mike. He doesn't drink tea, only water or milk - and Mother offered him milk" I tried my best to explain.

"You little liar! Your Mother wouldn't dream of asking that layabout in here, let alone his so called friend." Mother had gone into the kitchen while this was going on; I got up and shouted to her.

"Mother. You did invite them in didn't you? Please tell Dad." She slowly entered the living room drying her hands, without looking at me said.

"I said you could invite Mike here *one day*, not today though."

"Mother!" I screamed. *"That's not true and you know it!"* It was like a nightmare. I was horrified.

"Don't you dare speak to your Mother like that! I will not tolerate it, do you hear?" Dad yelled. I knew it was no use trying to reason with them. He went on.

"Bringing men in here for your Mother? What sort of woman do you think she is? That fellow is trying to take you down to his level. I'll just tell you one thing. So listen carefully! If you bring *any trouble* to this house, you'll be out through that door and no amount of pleading will make *any difference*. Is that clear?" He pushed his angry face so close to mine our noses were almost touching. *"Is-that-clear?"* he repeated. I just nodded feeling wretched.

I couldn't sleep that night. I relived the whole dreadful evening over and over. What a nightmare it had all been - and how will I ever face Mike and Tim again? Would they be insulted, angry or laugh it off? I had no idea what to expect.

Chapter Thirty Three
A Little Bit of Powder...

The following morning, Mother gave me breakfast in silence. I didn't speak either. I was so upset and preoccupied with the events of the previous night.

On reaching *Owen Owens'* I was met unexpectedly by the manageress Miss Gill.
"Oh. Good morning Lacey. I'm glad I've met you, I have some interesting news for you."
"The management would like you to do some evening classes on Skin Care. You'll be well paid and get commission on the products you sell. How does that sound?"
"Oh that sounds very good." I was excited by the idea, but *demonstrating* was something I'd never thought of doing. However, the extra money would be very useful. I felt apprehensive; would I be able to do it? The trauma of the previous night faded slightly. I was feeling excited with this new venture.

That same day, Amber, the receptionist, told me that Mike had rang to ask me for lunch. I was more than pleased, but also worried. What he would think of last night? Perhaps he'd say he didn't want to see me anymore?

I was panic stricken as I went to meet him. I ran towards him. He lifted me up and hugged me.
"Are you alright?" He looked concerned.
"I was so worried about you. I had no idea your parents could behave like that. You told me they could be difficult, but I had no idea, things were that bad. Tim and I were shocked at the silly accusations, but we were more worried about you. Are you ok really?" I was so relieved at Mike's concern.
"I wondered if you would ever want to see me again after last night?" Mike grabbed me close, planting kisses all over my face.
"You silly girl. How could you think such a thing. I love

A Dot's Life by Dorothy Buchanan

you. I'm not bothered at all what your parents say and do, that's their problem." My tears were now flowing. I felt so happy and relieved with Mikes words. We hugged each other for quite some time, while passers-by looked on.

During lunch I told Mike the news about the evening classes. Mike was thrilled by the idea.

"That's really good news!" He was very interested and excited. "This has all occurred at the right time for you, after the trauma of last night. You'll enjoy it and do well, you'll see!" Mike as usual was very reassuring. I began to look forward to this new venture and last nights' episode was slowly disappearing.

Things were still very strained at home. I tried to make peace and I told them about the night classes. But Mother and Dad seemed disinterested and made no comments.

Mike had given me so much support. I began to feel quite confident.

The day of the first demonstration arrived and I felt very apprehensive. I had lunch with Mike, which was lovely. He gave me the courage I badly needed, although I was still frightened. Miss Gill took me by taxi to the Adelphi hotel, where the demonstration was to be held. We set up the stage with the products and accessories. I would need I had a brand new uniform and wore my lovely red shoes. I was so busy for a time that I forgot what I would have to do! Miss Gill was very helpful giving me lots of advice, but my mind became a blank-

"Remember, these ladies are here to learn what you already know. Ask for volunteers, and then *choose a person you know you can transform.* Just chat about the products as you use them!" It all sounded so easy.

We had coffee and a light snack at the back of the stage. I could hear muffled voices from beyond the curtain. I was taking deep breaths, trying desperately to keep calm. So many thoughts were racing through my head. *Why had I agreed to do this?* Miss Gill realising my nerves were taking over, gave me a lengthy hug.

A Dot's Life by Dorothy Buchanan

"You'll be fine Lacey. Stop worrying. I have *complete* faith in you." I smiled weakly. Miss Gill patted me on the shoulder before she disappeared to address the audience.

Her introduction had come to an end. I was shaking with fear as I stood in the wings.

"Now let me introduce you to Miss Lacey." A lot of clapping went on as I slowly took my position on stage.

"Good evening ladies." I forced my face into a smile. "I hope you enjoy the evening." A sea of faces stared at me and the room had a heavy stillness. Taking a deep breath, I began gingerly explaining Rose Laird's products. A couple of times my voice wavered but it pleased me that nobody got up and walked out. Gradually I overcame the nervous beginning. The audience seemed interested (judging by the looks on their faces) and lots of hands went up when I asked for a volunteer. I took Miss Gills advice and chose a lady who looked pale but interesting. By now I was feeling confident; knowing that with some make-up, this lady would look *far more attractive*. The transformation was a big success the audience came up on stage to scrutinise the result with lots of them asking questions and buying the products I had used! Miss Gill was delighted she was selling lots of products and singing my praises. I was relieved and pleased that it had turned out so well, I couldn't wait to see Mike, who was waiting for me outside. I was overwhelmed by the evenings' events Mike caught me as I ran down the hotel steps

"It went well didn't it?" He said, hugging and kissing me. He was beaming.

"You look lovely! I could eat you!"

"Yes it was great!" I replied breathlessly

"Come on. Let's celebrate!" He said as we walked to a nearly pub.

Mike, always seem to know and say the right things. I kept looking at him, wondering if he could guess how much I thought of him; he was *so* understanding. I felt protected and loved. We sat holding hands and drinking our drinks.

"Come on. Tell me all about the evening." I told him everything, in short bursts. I was still full of nervous energy. He listened intently to everything,

"I knew you'd be fine." He kissed me again and again. It became a wonderful evening after all!

I did quite a few evening demonstrations after that. All arranged by Miss Gill. They were proving to be quite lucrative both for me and the beauty department. I lost my nervous beginnings and became a bit blasé about it all. Mike had given me such a lot of confidence and belief in myself.

Chapter Thirty Four
Steve Goes Fishing

Mike and I spent a lot of evenings together. My being out of the house seemed to suit Mother, as long as I was home by eleven o'clock. We either went to see a film, a play or just spend the evening in his flat which I think I enjoyed most - even Steve had become more friendly towards me.

The atmosphere at home was still frosty, Mike's name was never mentioned but they knew I was seeing him. It didn't bother me anymore. Mike was far more important to me now. We often talked about what we would do in the future; Mike had an idea to open a watchmakers' repair business, which he had trained for on leaving school in Ireland. He suggested I could run a mobile beauty business in the future. I thought this a good idea too, and I recalled of all the customers who had asked if I ever did home visits.

Our relationship was going so well. We were so close. We laughed a lot, having a similar sense of humour; sometimes quite wicked but not malicious.

Mike and Steve still attended a lot of political meeting, which I had no interest in, and lots of political friends called at the flat. When I was there I usually chose to make the tea and busied myself in the kitchen - which I enjoyed (pretending to be Mikes wife)! Their discussions were beyond me - talking of socialism, future societies, the Fabian society. Their discussions were often passionate and intense, but always amicable and respectful. I was glad to be spending so much time with Mike. Everything was going well and I felt very happy.

One of my regular clients asked if I could go to her house and do some make-up and, manicures, as one of her family were getting married on the following Sunday. I was surprised and delighted at the prospect! Sunday was an unusual day for a wedding, but they were Jewish and that was the custom.

A Dot's Life by Dorothy Buchanan

I arrived early at the house with my "Bag of Tricks" - some of the cosmetics were one's I'd borrowed from work. I did three facials, two manicures, two eyebrow trims. The house was full of guests - all very affluent, and could be future clients if and when I started on business my own.

They insisted I had my lunch there, smoked salmon, chopped liver and lots of delicacies it was a great experience, I also made almost ten pounds! I decided that I should think seriously about doing home visits.

Meanwhile Mike had managed to obtain a suitable place to do his watch-making repairs. It wasn't exactly a shop; it was the front area of a house which was converted for commercial use. It seemed ideal! It had a counter area and a workshop behind. Mike spent time decorating the shop; he had a plaque made with his name and occupation for the front entrance. He obtained a machine for cleaning watches and clocks, plus instruments etc. - the list seemed endless!

He worked hard getting everything just right - he even managed to secure some future work with a well known city jewellers. Mike was so engrossed with the shop, I hardly spent much time with him and I missed our evenings together. Sometimes I would visit him at the shop during my lunch hour, but the time went quickly.

One Wednesday, being my afternoon off, I decided to make a surprise meal for when he eventually arrived home. I knocked on the flat door, then realised I would have to get the key from the landlady. Before I rang her bell, Steve surprised me by opening the door. He grinned broadly.

"Hello Dot! Ernie isn't home yet." I disliked hearing Mike called *Ernie*, although it was his real name.

"I knew he wouldn't be home. I thought I would surprise him."

"I've just made a pot of tea, come and have a cup with me." I was really pleased by Steve's friendliness. This was the first time he'd spoken to me properly. I followed him into the kitchen which was full of steam and washing was bubbling away in an enamel bucket on the cooker. The sink was full of clothes. I'd never seen such a domestic scene there before. I sat myself on a work top, out of the way.

"You seem to be very organised with your washing." I tried to make conversation. He leaned across me to get a cup from the cupboard.

"I have to be!" Then he faced me. "My, you smell much nicer than this washing." I smiled.

"I work each day with lots of perfumes, so it's inevitable." I began to wonder if I had judged Steve wrongly.

"I expect you have to pamper a lot of empty headed middle class women all day – doesn't that annoy you?"

"No, it's a job I love doing." I couldn't understand why anyone would think it annoying? Steve didn't answer. I watched in silence as he finished the washing.

"More tea Dot?" he asked drying his hands.

"Yes, thank you." I was more than amazed with this change in Steve.

"Do you realise Steve, this is the first time you have ever had a conversation with me?" There was a long pause.

"Yes I'm aware of that."

"I thought you didn't approve of me?" He handed me the tea .

"You have been a very disturbing influence." He looked serious.

"A disturbing influence? How?"

"God, you're not thick, Dot! Surely you realise I can't bear to be in the same room as you!" I wasn't sure if it was some sort of joke, and gave a nervous laugh. Steve moved to where I was sitting, and put both his hands on my shoulders. His face close to mine. "Don't you realise Dot? I'm besotted with you!" With that he gently kissed my forehead and the tip of my nose. I pushed him away. I was flabbergasted.

"Don't be stupid Steve!" I shouted. "You know very well *I love Mike!*" Steve stepped back, looking very serious and carried on.

"Let's get this straight. I've never felt like this about *anyone*. I haven't come to this conclusion lightly. Over a long period

A Dot's Life by Dorothy Buchanan

now I've realised I'm in love with you - and this might come as a shock, but *I would like to marry you!*" I couldn't believe what I was hearing – *marry me?* So many thoughts were running around my head it was like a dream. I had to admit that I felt flattered. Here was this man who I thought disliked me, *now saying he wants to marry me!* I was stunned and sat open mouthed. Steve continued with what sounded like a rehearsed speech.

"Believe me. I've thought such a lot about you. I'm twenty seven and want to settle down. I know I have a great future politically, and I want a partner that will enhance my position - and *you would do just that!* You're *everything* I've ever dreamed of. You're perfect !" Wow! I was speechless. This was a surprise. I couldn't think how to reply, although I had to admit I did enjoy the flattery, it boosted my ego to high heaven!

Steve began hanging the washing on a maiden, I decided to go into the living room and wait for Mike. Steve caught my arm.

"I am sorry if I shocked you. I would like to talk to you at length, away from here, somewhere, anywhere please?" At that moment Mike came in. I was so relieved. But before I could run to him Steve whispered.

"Eleven o'clock .Princes Park. Sunday morning. Please be there." I didn't reply. I made an extra fuss of Mike. I felt guilty. He was surprised to see me.

"Did you miss me? I'm so pleased you came." He said hugging and kissing me.

Steve had made a meal of stew, my meal efforts were forgotten. Mike chatted throughout the meal about the progress of the shop. I felt very uncomfortable and kept glancing at Steve but he was as distant as usual. Eventually he went out, without glancing my way. Mike and I spent a lovely evening together. Lots of times I was tempted to tell him about Steve, but decided against it.

Nothing like this had ever happened to me before. I couldn't stop thinking about it. I kept going over and over the conversation. It felt exciting and also, I felt flattered. I would never have guessed that Steve could think of me the way he described.

Chapter Thirty Five
To Hook a Duck

Sunday was looming, I thought a lot about everything. One moment I decided to forget the whole episode, the next I was curious to hear what Steve would have to say. The element of danger fascinated me, and I decided to keep the appointment.

Princes Park was walking distance from home. It was a very wet morning. I kept wondering if Steve would be there. Part of me hoped he wouldn't be.

The entrance to the park had a long, tree-lined path with seats each side. The heavy rain had caused an atmospheric mist. Everywhere was deserted. It was then I noticed the solitary figure of Steve, under a large black umbrella.

He stood up waiting for me to reach him. Our umbrellas clashed and rain splattered over us; we laughed. Steve took my arm as we walked to a drier seat under a tree. It all seemed romantic, like a film set. I felt ashamed, while at the same time I was enjoying the intrigue. Steve took my hand and closed his eyes dramatically.

"At last! This is a dream realised. How often have I hoped for a moment like this." I couldn't comprehend how this aloof man could act in this way? I didn't know what to say. Steve continued to express his innermost emotions for me.

"I 'm aware you don't love me. But that could happen in time. Meanwhile, I have enough love for both of us. I know I could make you very happy." I knew I loved Mike *more than I could love anyone,* and could never think of Steve as anything other than an acquaintance, but my ego had taken over. I'd never experienced a situation like this before, and my emotions drifted between feeling guilty and deceitful, then excited and thrilled!

The rain was heavy. Streams of water dripped from our umbrellas as we sat huddled close - closer than I wanted to be. The park was deserted, except for one passer-by who gave us an odd glance. Steve

A Dot's Life by Dorothy Buchanan

held my hand kissing it now and again, whilst he talked non-stop.

"I would like to take you to Ireland to meet my family. They would like you very much, I'm sure of that." All these plans and compliments carried on. I was overwhelmed.

"Don't look so worried. I know this must be a shock to you, but I had to let you know my feelings, before you get too involved with Ernie! You are very young. I'm sure you must think you are in love, because he is a great person (and I'm very fond of him) but he wouldn't be right for you!" I began to panic, the situation was completely out of control! What I hoped would be a mild flirtation was becoming ridiculous! I felt angry – with Steve and with myself for being there!

"Look Steve, whatever you think, I *am in love with Ernie*, I have known him long enough to make up my mind. Whatever you say or think I shall never change my mind. So let's forget it. Come on, let's go." Steve looked pained and sighed. We left the park in silence. I made my way home feeling very puzzled and guilty. Steve - a stranger last week - now he's talking of a future together!

I saw Mike later that afternoon I felt so guilty and badly wanted to tell him everything, but I knew I daren't. Mike was working hard at his shop and getting a lot of work. He was thrilled everything was going well.

We made plans for the coming week, and decided to go and see a continental film, showing in Wallasey across the river - we would take the ferry across the Mersey. We often went to see films locally, but I had never seen a continental film (with subtitles) before. The last film we saw was *"Blood and Sand"* starring one of my favourites - Tyrone Power. I was pleased and relieved we wouldn't be spending many evenings at the flat. I didn't want to see Steve.

"I'll meet you from work, and then we could have a quick bite to eat and be in good time for the full programme," said Mike.

The cinema was small, more like a church hall, with individual chairs. The film was unusual and interesting; it had the unusual title *"The sheep with six legs."* We both enjoyed the evening very much, and on the way home, Mike told me Steve was moving to a flat of his own, a couple of doors away.

A Dot's Life by Dorothy Buchanan

"It's good news for us, we will have the flat to ourselves," he said hugging and kissing me. I was relieved and puzzled as to why Steve had left.

I was happier than I ever thought possible. Mike was all I could have wished for; loving, thoughtful, and such fun to be with! Everything was perfect. Mother and Dad knew I was spending a lot of time with Mike now, but they neither expressed approval or disapproval.

Lots of times I took David to the flat, he was older now and enjoyed browsing through the numerous books Mike had. David also enjoyed a few trips which Tim offered us in his car.

One evening, on my way to see Mike I was surprised when Steve caught up with me he was on his way home, I hadn't seen him since that morning in the park. He gave me a friendly smile. I felt a bit uncomfortable.

"Hello dot. How are you?"

"Fine. Thanks, and you?" I tried to sound casual.

"I'm ok. I've been busy decorating my flat. Come and have a look." We'd reached his front door. I was pleased he just seemed civil and friendly. I followed him in, his flat was on the first floor. It was far smaller than I had imagined, but very tastefully decorated.

"It's good isn't it?" Steve seemed pleased and different to when I last saw him.

"Sit down. I'll make you a cup of tea. The kettle won't take long."

"Oh, thank you. Yes, I think your flat is ideal. You've made it very comfortable." Steve put two cups of tea on a tray and placed them on the divan bed.

"Come and sit here." He patted a place beside him. We drank our tea in silence, and then he threw his arms around me tightly. "This is what I have dreamed of for so long. You know I've never stopped loving you!"

"Steve, what on earth are you doing! I told you before I love Ernie and always will. You're wasting your time and mine. I'm going" I tried to release myself from his grip but he pushed me

A Dot's Life by Dorothy Buchanan

across the bed and attempted to kiss me, as we struggled there was a tap on the door and Mike came in! I was horrified. Steve gasped. I quickly got up, and straightened my hair.

"What the hell is going on?" shouted Mike looking very angry. Steve quickly got to his feet, I froze rooted to the spot

"Look Ernie," Steve began, looking somewhat uncomfortable.

"Carry on, I'm listening," said Mike, looking first at me, then Steve.

"Mike, this is not what it looks like," I mumbled.

"Dot was only here to see my flat. I took advantage of the situation and tried to kiss her, that's all." He looked almost pleased with his quick explanation.

"Come on both of you. I want to know the truth." Mike was really annoyed now

"Ok, this is the situation," Steve began. "You'll be surprised to learn that I think a lot of Dot; in fact *I believe I'm in love with her!* It upset me to see you both together. *That's the reason I moved flat.* I've told Dot, and asked her to make sure it was *you* that she really wanted to be with." Mike's mouth dropped in amazement.

"You never even spoke to Dot! How could you fall in love with someone you didn't even know?" I panicked. I didn't want Steve to tell him I had met him in the park!

"Mike, I met Steve on my way to see you. He asked me to see his flat. That's why I'm here. Just before you came in, he'd told me how much he thought of me. Then he tried to kiss me. I made it clear that I loved you and I tried to get away from him." With that burst of explanation, I rushed over to Mike and grabbed his arm. "Honestly. That's all that happened." Mike studied me then put his arm around me.

"I understand Dot. Just forget this ever happened."

"I can't believe your behaviour Steve. I'm quite disgusted to think you would try such a cheap trick."

"As for being in love, that is so ridiculous you don't even know Dot" Steve looked uncomfortable and began washing the dishes.

"Come on Dot. Let's go." Mike and I rushed out of the flat. I was so relieved it had ended much better than I anticipated.

Back at the flat Mike kept talking about Steve and how amazed he was by his behaviour.

"He's never, ever shown any interest in you - or any other females that I know of. He's so wrapped up with the political scene to have much social life, but he obviously found you irresistible! I can understand that!" He gave me a hug. The evening became very eventful. We talked at length about our future together; our hopes, dreams and plans for the future. It was magical. We talked seriously about getting married. This was the first time we'd talked in this way.

"We'll get married as soon as you are twenty one, how does that sound?" We decided on that because we knew Mother and Dad would not agree to anything sooner. I was so happy. we spent the rest of the evening hugging and kissing and saying how much we loved each other, making huge plans - it was wonderful.

Chapter Thirty Six
The Lunch Box

The following week while we were having lunch together in the café opposite *Owen Owens'* Mike said he had a surprise for me.

"What sort of surprise?" I was puzzled.

"Wait until we've had our lunch," he replied, winking. I finished my meal in no time. Mike took a ring box out of his pocket, watching my reaction closely. He opened the box slowly. I was so surprised and excited. I couldn't believe my eyes a lovely square shaped blue-green stone gleamed with twinkling stones each side. I gasped,

"It's beautiful!" I had never seen a ring like it!

"It's a Zircon," Mike explained. He took my hand, kissed it, then placed the ring on my engagement finger. I couldn't speak - it was lovely! He leaned over the table and cupped my face in his hands and kissed me.

"It's not the usual diamond engagement ring, but it's the best I can manage at this moment. We will have to save up to get a flat soon - I hope you'll understand? It does have diamonds each side of the stone, at least."

"Oh I don't care about diamonds. This is the *loveliest ring I've ever seen.*" I sat for quite some time admiring my outstretched hand. I felt so special. We kissed and hugged each other oblivious of the other diners. I ran back to work to show the girls.

"I'm engaged," I announced.

They all took a great interest in my ring, but some looked quizzical

"I've never seen an engagement ring without it been diamonds!"

"It's a lovely ring, and quite unusual," said another.

"I know it's not the usual type of engagement ring, but it means everything to me and I'm very happy with it." I felt a bit let down with their reactions, but I soon forgot them when I thought of Mike and I being married.

I had a similar reaction when I got home,

"Mike and I got engaged today." I wanted to tell everyone.

"Really? Where is your ring?" She asked rather sarcastically. I thrust my left hand under her nose

She took a quick look and snorted, "What sort of ring is that? It looks like one you would get in Woolworths?"

"I know it's not the usual engagement ring with diamonds, but *I'm* delighted with it!"

Further copies of **A Dot's Life**
can be ordered directly from **www.lulu.com**

Printed in Great Britain
by Amazon.co.uk, Ltd.,
Marston Gate.